Your Moment Is Now

*You Matter!
What is your story?

Much Love,
Lu Ann*

Your Moment Is Now

Memoirs of God's Love

Lu Ann Topovski

Copyright © 2020 by Lu Ann Topovski.

Library of Congress Control Number: 2020906928
ISBN: Hardcover   978-1-7960-9703-0
             Softcover   978-1-7960-9702-3
             eBook   978-1-7960-9701-6

All rights reserved. No part of this book may be reproduced or transmitted in any form or by any means, electronic or mechanical, including photocopying, recording, or by any information storage and retrieval system, without permission in writing from the copyright owner.

Any people depicted in stock imagery provided by Getty Images are models, and such images are being used for illustrative purposes only.
Certain stock imagery © Getty Images.

Scripture quotations marked NIV are taken from the Holy Bible, New International Version®. NIV®. Copyright © 1973, 1978, 1984 by International Bible Society. Used by permission of Zondervan. All rights reserved. [Biblica]

Scripture quotations are from the ESV® Bible (The Holy Bible, English Standard Version®), copyright © 2001 by Crossway, a publishing ministry of Good News Publishers. Used by permission. All rights reserved.

Scripture quotations marked AMP are from The Amplified Bible, Old Testament copyright © 1965, 1987 by the Zondervan Corporation. The Amplified Bible, New Testament copyright © 1954, 1958, 1987 by The Lockman Foundation. Used by permission. All rights reserved.

Scripture quotations marked KJV are from the Holy Bible, King James Version (Authorized Version). First published in 1611. Quoted from the KJV Classic Reference Bible, Copyright © 1983 by The Zondervan Corporation.

Scripture quotations marked NKJV are taken from the New King James Version. Copyright © 1982 by Thomas Nelson, Inc. Used by permission. All rights reserved.

Scripture quotations marked HCSB are from the Holman Christian Standard Bible®. HCSB®. Copyright ©1999, 2000, 2002, 2003 by Holman Bible Publishers. Used by permission. Holman Christian Standard Bible®, Holman CSB®, and HCSB® are federally registered trademarks of Holman Bible Publishers

Scripture quotations marked NLT are taken from the Holy Bible, New Living Translation, copyright © 1996, 2004, 2007. Used by permission of Tyndale House Publishers, Inc. Carol Stream, Illinois 60188. All rights reserved. Website

Printed in the United States of America

Rev. date: 05/01/2020

To order additional copies of this book, contact:
Xlibris
1-888-795-4274
www.Xlibris.com
Orders@Xlibris.com

CONTENTS

Story	Name	Page
1	Megan Jagger	1
2	Royel and Olivia Jones	9
3	Pastor Ryan Smith	18
4	Ashley Boreman	22
5	Deon Howard	28
6	Brittany R. Fikes	30
7	Greg Massaro	32
8	Bishop Cor-re-don Rogers	34
9	Lydia Sibbalds	40
10	Anonymous	44
11	Pamela D. Brinkley	48
12	Tanya Hastings Blalock	52
13	Bishop Dr. Gregory Draper	55
14	Mandy Nippert	57
15	Pearl Basinger	62
16	Sha'ri D. Birchfield	64
17	Ashlee Wortz	68
18	David Schuster	72
19	Johnson (John) Noel	80
20	Don Johnson	82
21	Antoinette Roberts	89
22	Meredith Hancock (†)	93
23	George O. Topovski	101
24	Joel Sibbalds	107

25	Juanita Teasley	110
26	LaKesha Cunningham	113
27	Jamal McClendon	116
28	Candace Williams	118
29	Rhonda Stewart	126
30	Sabrina Stump	131
31	Terri Black	138
32	Don Kister	140
33	Jessica and Madison Pritt	142
34	Lynnette Fowler	148
35	Trang Le	150
36	Ward Edinger	152
37	Chris Smith	153
38	Afton Hill	155
39	Kathy Weitzel Christian	158
40	Marty Lotito	160
41	Joe Carfelli	164
42	Joshua Bechtel	169
43	Christy Jackson	178
44	Pastor Bill Purvis	189
45	Lu Ann Topovski	200

AUTHOR'S NOTE

ALL STORIES SHARED within this book came from the most sacred part of each individual soul. In the depths of despair and then into the light of hope; redemption, healing and life were felt by all. Some of these stories have been traumatizing. Yet these amazing Christians kept focused on their faith, which is where their strength and courage came from. Some have faced death. Others have died and come back to life. It was with their firm foundation in Christ, and the power of God, that they overcame personal tragedies. Now they courageously share their stories within this book.

These testimonials are a gift to us. They will speak to everyone reading this book, or those who have sought confirmation within their own journey. Our hope is that others can be led to Christ by seeing the impact God has had on individual lives. We would like to dedicate this book, in part, to those who shared their testimonies, as well as their families. We know that hardship is felt within the family system, not just the one fighting the personal battle.

As a way of giving back, ten percent of the profits of this book will go to the individual story authors, or to their family, to honor them.

I am sad to report that, during the editing of this book, one of our storytellers, Meredith Hancock, passed away before the publication of this book. Meredith was always strong and helpful to those who needed her. Our hearts and prayers are with Meredith's family.

PERSONAL DEDICATION

THIS BOOK IS dedicated to all who are searching for a sign that God is real. You might not have had these experiences yourself, but by having faith, even as small as a mustard seed, you can move what might seem to be a mountain in front of you. May you feel the strength and presence of the Holy Spirit as you read, and may you say to your mountain, "Move!"

Lu Ann Topovski, M.Div, MBA

INTRODUCTION

FAITH IS NOT always easy. Sometimes it takes more energy and strength to have faith than to not have any at all. Faith can be a burden when it gets in the way of our personal desires or when we must wait for an answer. Ultimately, faith is believing in the kingdom of God and his governmental rule over the earth's cursed system. When we have faith in God's kingdom principles, life becomes manageable and sustainable. In fact, when we "seek first the kingdom of God and his righteousness, all these things are added unto [us]" (Matthew 6:33 NIV). Is it easy? Not always. This is when our faith kicks in—or grows. Clinging to God's promises is important every day.

Faith is one of the gifts of the Holy Spirt. Sometimes when traumatic things happen in our lives, it is the impartation of faith by the Holy Spirit that helps us get through the day, week, or month. We know at some level it is not us. Sometimes, we admit when it's God's intervention that got us through, gave us strength, or miraculously did something in the natural realm that changed our life. When hundreds of people are praying for us, we feel the presence and peace of God. It's incredible and, sometimes, indescribable.

Some people don't like to go to that place in their thinking. In fact, faith is a scary place for many people. It just doesn't make sense. Some say, "Faith is a relationship with Jesus." Others say, "What does that mean?"

The stories you are about to read are all about personal faith journeys from individuals who chose to take a leap of faith and believe in God through their life situations. We hope these stories will inspire you and be prepared; many might bring you to tears.

These memoires are written and shared authentically by people who trusted God through personal trials. We are all unique and interesting individual beings. We laugh, cry, get excited, and get angry. Our range of emotions vary with circumstances, but it is often our faith in God that pulls us through events that are life-changing or even life-threatening.

As you read through each story, you might feel the emotion felt by the individuals sharing their story. It is because your soul will empathize with their soul and their life event. That means it might be transforming for you. It is clear to us that in these stories God intervened. These individual situations have no other explanation except God's hand of intervention. *To God be the glory!*

> **From everyone who has been given much, much will be required; and from the one who has been entrusted with much, even more will be expected.**
>
> **—Luke 12:48 CSB**

STORY 1

Megan Jagger

You Really Want a Donkey?

I CANNOT TELL YOU how many times or how many ways, in the last five years, I have answered this question. The fact is, I can give you the same answer all day long. Most people will not be able to understand unless they have, at some time in their life, had no choice but to blindly follow in faith, as well as share quality time with a long-eared beast of burden.

The first person to question this never-before discussed topic was my husband of forty years. We had recently purchased his father's home in the Poconos out of the estate. This was a plan I was not totally supportive of. My husband, Bill, had just cleaned thirty-five years of JUNK out of the stalls in the barn and called me to see his accomplishment. I looked in the stalls and proclaimed, "Oh yay, we can get donkeys!"

He just looked at me like I was an alien dropped into his very responsible, always practical, and never-not-logical-thinking wife's body. He picked his chin up off the floor and very cautiously proceeded with this conversation. "Why do you want a donkey?" came next. I immediately responded, "Because I do."

This would be the juncture in all our conversations, that after forty years this man has learned to pause and decide if he would like to be right or if he would like to be happy. Evidently, he was still not sure if his wife had been abducted by aliens, but he still wanted to be happy. He asked a few more questions as to care, feeding, cost, etc. I had immediate responses to all questions. I do not know why. This was not an endeavor I had spent years planning, thinking, or dreaming about. Finally, staying happy won out, and he conceded we could go LOOK at ONE donkey. We came home with three, soon to be four: two miniature donkeys named Nugget and Snickers, as well as a pregnant standard-size donkey named Wilma. Wilma gave birth to Waffles a couple months into this venture.

My adult life, as most folks can say, has not always been easy. When we were married, there was not one person who knew either my husband or me who gave our marriage the life span of a carton of milk. We were quite literally homeless, with no support system whatsoever. I was still in school and my husband was recently home from Vietnam—with all the baggage he brought with him. Then children came into the picture. Life was in every aspect dysfunctional and overwhelming, the effects of which started to unravel us in drastic ways. He had multiple issues after his days in the service. I was fully engrossed in getting through school and finding a way to support us. As of today, neither one of us knows how we made it through this period of our lives as individuals, let alone as a couple and a soon-to-be young family.

One day at a time—sometimes one minute at a time—life began dumping situations that created an absolute need to pull together in order to survive and move forward in very small, wobbling baby steps. For years we were able to exist in this survival mode. I have no idea how or why. I was never not grateful or hopeful or completely believing that if we could stick together and keep pushing forward, we would get through. I did not know where I expected or wanted us to go. I was too busy surviving. Looking back, it was blind faith. I know it now. Only the Lord could have kept us alive, let alone out of jail, safe, and a family unit in whatever definition you might apply.

This went on day by day in the small county my husband had been raised in. After about fifteen years we got a call from his mother. She was catastrophically ill and needed our help. She now lived in Florida. I was aware we needed to make a geographic change. We had gotten ourselves as far as we could living in an economically depressed part of the country where the baggage of several past generations of family followed us everywhere. With much discussion and agonizing we packed up our family—and our lives—and headed to Florida. This was one of the best decisions we ever made. We started anew. The children were in good schools, we had good jobs, and for the first time, we felt as if we could breathe and grow.

> **I did not know where I expected or wanted us to go. I was too busy surviving. Looking back, it was blind faith. I know it now.**

Then came the No-Name Storm. This was an early spring storm that came from nowhere and literally took out most of the west coast of central Florida. We had five feet of saltwater in the home we were renting. We lost two cars and every material thing we owned. The home we were renting while our house was under construction was condemned, and we could not live in it for the remaining three months we needed until our home was completed.

One week later, my husband's mother died of breast cancer. We were still homeless and unable to work because we had nothing. No cars, no clothes, no place to live, again no functional external support system. Depression does not begin to cover this level of loss. Then out of the blue, while we were working on cleaning up of the mess, three pick-up trucks pulled up to the house. They were parents from our children's Little League team. They came and took all the laundry. I am talking a two-car garage filled three feet deep with wet, smelly, moldy clothes and bed linens. They left and came back a few hours later. It was all washed, dried, folded, and on hangers. I cried. I still cry when I think back on all the little acts of kindness that kept us hopeful throughout that time.

Slowly, with much spiritual, emotional, and physical help, the family recovered both inside and out from the losses of that year. The devastation required changes in every aspect of our lives that we thought we would never need to make. Both of us had lost employment as our places of employment were indefinitely closed due to the storm damages. We had a new house to pay for and our children were now teens in need of parenting more than ever.

I started back to school to work on a master's degree. My husband hit the road as a full-time truck driver. This essentially left me as a single parent while working full time and going to school as well. It took my husband very far away from his sole support system in life. On bad days we had time to grieve and wonder how such a fleeting act of nature could create such ongoing, never-ending sacrifice. On good days we were just fully absorbed in getting through the day because we were so immersed in the day to day of survival again.

We were too engrossed in our own pain to see that, once again our foundation was a house of cards. It did not take long before that house began to shake and crumble. The children were struggling in school, and the family time we could muster was tenuous and full of bickering. The entire family was living day to day waiting for the next shoe to fall. The only ones who couldn't see it was us. We did, by the grace of God, find our way to a wonderful counselor who helped us heal as a family. This came from the suggestion of our attorney who we needed to help us resolve the fallout of the devastation. Once again, we were moving forward. The kids settled down, and my husband and I came to terms with the career choices necessary for us to support ourselves financially. We were even functioning well through the work travel and time apart as a couple.

Life was swimming along. We had recovered from our last round of devastation. I finished school and found a good position. The trucking business was doing well. The children were now in college, and the light at the end of the tunnel, for the first time in a long time, had started to look like an actual light, not a train. We sold the home we built on the Gulf of Mexico, as the children were slowly inching out the door and it was time to downsize some. We wanted to get off the water with me home alone much of the time. We did not know how or why, but we had survived once again by not having time to question the journey but by putting one foot in front of the other. We once again felt we had much to be grateful for.

We had almost made it through the whole Y2K hysteria unscathed when our oldest daughter announced she and her live-in significant other were expecting. She was too young, and they were too everything else wrong for this plan to ever work—this was my initial reaction. However, so were we. Now here we were, having this same conversation about one of our children. We decided to be quietly supportive, as it was not for us to judge. Long story short, our daughter and grandchild spent until 2016 living in our downsized semiretirement home that was too small.

At the time, I thought the worst of all my trials to date were still to come when our daughter and granddaughter moved in. In retrospect, I am not sure I could have faced life some days if not for the fact that the two of them needed me not to fall apart. Today I can say, I would not have traded that time with either of them for any material thing.

Because of our experience, both my husband and I always felt strongly about doing what we could for storm victims. To this end, he was a FEMA first responder for over sixteen storms, and I worked as a Red Cross nurse. In 2008 he was just off Katrina, Rita, and Wilma when he ruptured a disc in his back and needed to be flown home to Florida from Texas for emergency back surgery. All went well, but the neurosurgeon told him "No more driving the truck" as a post-operative restriction. Now we have a cardiologist from a failed pre-operative cardiac catheterization and a neurosurgeon saying "No more driving the truck!" Did he listen? NO! Back to work he went. That lasted for about two more years when he slipped on ice and ruptured a quad tendon in his right leg and spent four months totally non-weight-bearing. THEN he stopped driving the truck! The trucking business was sold, and he was home for good.

Please try to picture Animal from the Muppets living in your house. That was life with a person who lived and worked in solitary confinement on wheels for a prolonged time. I promise you, I worked sixty plus hours a week during this time because I needed the rest.

During the process of filing for disability, his cardiac condition was resurrected. More tests were done, and it was determined his cardiac condition was due to Agent Orange exposure while he was in Vietnam. He was now not only disabled by Social Security but by the military as well.

I am not sure if some people understand the emotional devastation of becoming disabled. It is not only that you are not earning a paycheck anymore. It is that you can no longer do what you do to support your family. You are now dependent on others, and your working life is over well before you planned it to be. I would never have understood the feeling of total uselessness had I not watched it happen to someone so close to me.

> This was an opportunity to parlay a modest inheritance into not only a secure retirement income for us but unencumbered homes for the next two generations of our family. Once again, we had obediently followed.

While we were riding the wave of "wait and see" with my husband's disability, I lost a generation of family. My father, all my aunts and uncles, ending with my father-in-law being diagnosed with end-stage lung cancer, with about three months to live. My husband promptly dispatched himself to Pennsylvania to support his father through this terrible process, as there really was no other family able to help. The three months turned into three very long, emotionally abusive years. During this time, my husband's health was declining. His pulse was decreasing to a dangerously low rate, causing him to pass out with no warning. While in the VA hospital in Scranton, he went into cardiac arrest. He was revived and today will tell you he is "battery operated." He has a pacemaker, and I am so grateful to say, he is largely fine. This was by far the hardest trial yet for all of us.

The result of this whole emotional ordeal was, we ended up with the family homestead in Pennsylvania. This was an opportunity to parlay a modest inheritance into not only a secure retirement income for us but unencumbered homes for the next two generations of our family. Once again, we had obediently followed.

That house in Pennsylvania has been a source of contention with me from day 1. It brought nothing but memories of past pain and trial for me but, now we had it. It had not been cleaned in over fifteen years because no one had been allowed to touch anything in the house. It had antique tractors in varying state of repair lying all over the place. I felt like I was driving into the movie set from *Deliverance* when I pulled up to the place. The geographic location is remote and not friendly for me, but now we owned it. I could go on with the misery, or I could get on with life. I chose getting on with life.

The house was emptied, cleaned, and painted. The pool was opened for the first time in years. The pool house was converted to a guest cabin and is now on Airbnb so others can enjoy our little piece of tranquility when family is not using it. The deer and wildlife were getting fed out in the woods daily. We acquired chickens, stocked the trout stream, and replenished the game birds. The garden was planted with vegetables growing in it. Hanging plants of petunias and impatiens were hung all around the house, decks, and pool. The house was starting to look happy for the very first time since I could remember.

Then the children, grandchildren, nieces, and nephews started planning vacations up to the Poconos. We make a yearly pilgrimage to the county fair, where the grandchildren enter a vegetable they helped grow or a jar of jelly they help make with the highlight being watching Papa and Dad in the antique tractor pull. They have started calling it their "Memory Maker."

On the day the barn finally got cleaned out, I promise you, I did not get up in the morning planning on owning eight donkeys. I can tell you donkeys are a little like potato chips. You can't have just one.

The only reason I can tell you my desire for wanting donkeys in my life always is, they make me smile and remind me every day that faith is the environment of blessings and miracles. They provide me tangible proof

Donkey hugs are the BEST!

that without the gift of faith, I would enjoy not one of the blessings in my life today. They are the most complete example of faith and goodness I have ever come across. There is not a day that goes by they do not greet us with love, treat us with kindness, and wait with never-ending faith that we will return to them just so they can love us some more. They teach me on such a basic level that of all the trials I have encountered and those I have yet to encounter, I must be prepared to follow God's instructions, demonstrate my faith, and worship from my heart.

STORY 2

Royel and Olivia Jones

Mother's Version

DECEMBER 22, 2002, was a day I will never forget. I was a stay at home mom for my two beautiful girls, Khyla and Olivia. I believe God prepared me, as a stay-at-home mom, for what was about to happen to my family.

On this night, we had Olivia in our bed because she had not been feeling well. She had stopped walking and was complaining of her ankle hurting. We could not get her shoe on because she would cry out. We took her to many foot doctors to figure out what was going on with her ankle. We could not tell anything was wrong with her ankle by looking at it, but clearly, she was hurting. The doctors took many x-rays and scans to see if they could find the answer. All x-rays and scans came back as if everything looked good. But on this night, she woke up crying that her stomach hurt. I knew she was not constipated or hungry. She had been on several medications because she kept getting ear infections. I looked at my husband and said, "We need to get her to the hospital." I had a feeling it was something more.

We took her to the children's hospital ER in Columbus, Ohio, the best hospital in Ohio for children. They took us back to a room. We had to carry her everywhere because the pain was causing her to not want to walk. This was hard for her to understand because she knew she used to walk. She would see other kids running and playing but she had to be carried or would crawl. It broke my heart.

The doctors were not sure what was going on with her, so they started out with a blood test. They had given her some morphine to help with the pain. She ended up falling asleep in the bed. I kept thinking morphine is a strong drug to give a kid. I sang softly in her ear while rubbing her curly hair. She loved the songs, "You Are My Sunshine" and "Jesus Loves Me." The doctor came back to the room and told us she had leukemia.

> The pain she was having with her ankle and stomach was from the leukemia cells attacking her ankle and spleen.

The pain she was having with her ankle and stomach was from the leukemia cells attacking her ankle and spleen. Also, the several ear infections she was getting were from her white blood cells being so low. She could not fight off all the infections. She was considered high-risk. The doctors stated she would have made it for only a couple months if we had waited any longer. The doctor said we would be admitted, and we would meet the hematology group in morning. It was the middle of the night, and we were finally in our room. I remember making that phone call to my mom, who was watching Khyla, and told her Olivia had leukemia. That was so hard to say out loud.

So keep in mind this was only a few days away from Christmas, which was the last thing on my mind. However, our great family and friends took Khyla out and brought Olivia back a pretty pink princess tree with matching ornaments. My mom finished wrapping all the gifts at home that I bought them for Christmas. Thank goodness I was not a procrastinator when it came to getting ready for Christmas. She brought the gifts down to the hospital the next day, which would have been Christmas Eve.

We had asked a family friend who was a pastor to come visit her. That day, she had to have surgery to insert the port in her upper chest so they would not have to poke and prod at her to find veins for medicines or blood withdrawals/transfusions. We were told to be honest with her about anything being done to her by the doctors so she would trust us and them. We had explained to her that she would have surgery to insert the port and the reason why. She didn't really understand at the age of three, but she was a very smart girl. When she woke up from surgery, they called us to come back because she would not calm down. I walked in and saw she was awake and scared.

She had tape on her neck and chest. The first thing she asked me was "What was on my neck?" I did not realize she would have two incisions. My heart ached because she couldn't turn her head a certain way because of the tape. When we finally got her back to her room, the pastor was there waiting. We got her settled into her bed, and an aide pulling a wagon full of toys and games came in to ask her to pick something out. All she said was, "I want to ride in the wagon."

> We got her settled into her bed and an aide pulling a wagon full of toys and games came in to ask her to pick something out. All she said was, "I want to ride in the wagon."

The pastor stayed and prayed over her and then left so we could get her into a wagon for a ride. That night was Christmas Eve, and the hospital allowed Khyla to stay in the room so we could wake up as a family. Our friends, who attend the church of that pastor, said he had told the story of visiting a child in the hospital. She could have picked any toy out of the wagon, but all she wanted was a simple wagon ride. It is true; sometimes it is that simple.

The next morning, we woke up to presents under the pink princess Christmas tree. We told the girls, "Santa always knows where you are." It was the best day we could have had at that time. Our families and friends gave up their day to come visit with us. We felt so loved.

I called a friend of mine whom I worked with at JFS to ask her to pray for Olivia. She said, "Of course!" She called me later and wanted to tell me a person who goes to the church called her. He said, God had told him that the little girl would be OK. That meant so much to know people you do not know are praying for you and God answers.

After several meetings with the doctors and in such a short time, we learned what we had to do to make her better. She had her own team of doctors and nurses. They were all amazing. Her disease was called acute lymphoblastic leukemia a.k.a. ALL, which we took as a blessing.

The other type would have been much worse. We took on a positive attitude and knew it was going to be OK. We had our faith.

After two weeks of taking only steroids, Olivia was diagnosed to be leukemia-free. The doctors said they were expecting to see a decrease, but for her to be leukemia-free was surprising. They did not see this in any case for anyone in the past. I knew why. It was God. I was hoping to be done and that she was cured. But the doctors informed us that it is important to finish out the 2½ years of treatment to make sure it stays gone.

Our first week of visits to the clinic after being released from the hospital were a whirlwind. She had to go to the clinic at first, three times a week. We did not know what to expect or how it worked. We saw a lot of new medical staff and kids in the same predicament. I remember it being very crowded in the waiting room. We had brought a backpack, plus we had coats to carry because it was winter. I had my purse, but all I was focused on was making her comfortable.

When they finally called us back, we gathered our things and headed back to the room with chairs and IV stands. They got her all hooked up and started medications. Some of the medications took a long time to give. They had to go slowly into her tiny body.

We were sitting there for about an hour and I thought, *Where is my purse?* I looked around and we could not find it. I went out in the waiting room, which was empty by that time, but I could not find my purse. I went up to the receptionist and asked if anyone turned in a purse to the desk. She said no. They called security to come take a report, but all I wanted to do was get back in the room with Olivia. I wasn't thinking of my driver's license or social security card. Plus there was a wad of cash my husband's coworkers collected to help us with gas and food for our many trips to doctor appointments. I still did not care.

There was a time when I thought about money all the time, but that day, I did not think about it. All I wanted was my baby to be healthy. You cannot buy health. And now that I had been through this, I valued it more than before. The only important thing was my family. Material things were not meaningful anymore. I felt in my heart that whoever took my purse that day must have needed the money more than us.

They did find my purse in a trash can near a bathroom in a hallway. Everything was in there except for the cash.

I never let Olivia see me upset or scared. I would cry in the shower, car, and even cleaning out the horse stall. Our horse Suzie was such a great listener. She heard me talk to God a lot. I never questioned God. I believe we are in seasons in our lives for some reason. Only he knows what is going on. He will never leave; he will be beside us through all the nightmares.

I feel it made her and us stronger. She was such a brave little girl. I remember thinking I don't know if I could be that brave. Of course, being young helped—she did not understand the severity of what she was going through. She would ask occasionally what was going on, but our answer was to get her better. I knew she knew God was with her.

She missed out on things like playing outside. We had to be careful because if she would breathe something in, that normally you or I could fight off, her little body might not be able to fight off, and she could come down with pneumonia. Anytime she had a fever, we had to admit her to the hospital to make sure there was no infection in her port. If that happened, the infection could go straight to her heart. We were very careful in who and what she was around. Washing hands all the time became the norm. We carried wet wipes wherever we went. We could never be too careful.

The moment came when she could finally walk again. We wanted to get her out of the house, so we decided to go see Grandma Bailey at her elderly apartment complex. My girls love going to visit her. Grandma Bailey was a Christian woman and lived her life according to the Bible. She kept a picture of Olivia in her Bible for protection. Olivia was going through physical therapy to retrain her muscles to walk. It was going slow, but we knew it would work.

Grandma Bailey wanted Olivia to sit on her lap, so we sat her there. She was hugging her so tightly, but I could see she was whispering something in Olivia's

> **Suddenly, Olivia climbed down off her lap and started walking. Of course, it was not pretty, but she had never initiated it before on her own. She had a huge smile on her face, and we were all crying and clapping. She just kept walking everywhere.**

ear. Suddenly, Olivia climbed down off her lap and started walking. Of course, it was not pretty, but she had never initiated it before on her own. She had a huge smile on her face, and we were all crying and clapping. She just kept walking everywhere. The apartment was tiny, so we took her out in the long hallway to walk. Her sister Khyla was only six at the time but was so excited for her. I know in my heart when Grandma Bailey was whispering in her ear it was from God.

We had many scares through this process. She had several spinal taps, where they withdrew fluid and then injected chemo meds back into her spine. They did this so that just in case the leukemia came back, it would not be in her spinal fluid. The medicine that would normally relax a person (such as Versed, fentanyl, and such) would just make her angry. The nurses said sometimes kids would see you as monster.

Olivia needed to be still during this process because they were working with the spine and nerves. We as parents could be with her in the procedure, but I could not take it. My husband would go with her. I remember standing outside the room and hearing Code Blue go off. All these doctors and nurses came running into the room. I was terrified. She sucked too much of the gas down into her lungs. My husband said her lips started turning blue, and he was getting upset. We had to be careful days after the procedure. The doctors were concerned she would develop pneumonia. God is good though, and she was fine.

As a nineteen-year-old woman now, she does not remember all the horrific things that happened to her during that season in her life. I don't want her to remember. But I do know remembering is a part of her healing and understanding of what she went through and why. We have talked about this time in our lives and will continue talking about it. It makes her who she is today. She is a very smart, funny, and beautiful woman whom I admire. She has a scar on her chest that people can sometimes see, and she is not afraid to show it. If someone asks, she proudly explains what she went through to have that scar.

Both of my girls are in college now. Olivia and her sister Khyla have written many papers for school about this disease. I feel that because we went through this as a family, both of my girls hope to be some part of the medical field.

Olivia is very healthy now. She will continue to go back to the children's hospital for checkups every year for the rest of her life. It will help them with studies on the aftereffects on a patient finished in taking medicines. Many of these medicines have long-term effects on the body. I am glad they keep in such good contact with patients. This disease has a high rate of being cured.

Daughter's Version

Below is the story through Olivia's eyes. A paper written for Honors English, May 1, 2016, when she was sixteen-year-old.

My Journey through Leukemia

The pitter-patter of little feet. The pitter-patter of little feet is the sweetest sound a parent could hear. Then it stops. One day you are a parent of a toddler, and the next day you are the parent of a toddler with leukemia. That was my parents' perspective on my story, and this essay is all about mine.

I was three years old when I was diagnosed with acute lymphoblastic leukemia (ALL). My parents became concerned when I developed severe stomach and ankle pain. The pain in my ankle became so relentless that it quickly escalated from me not putting on my shoes, and next I completely stopped walking. I had to complete nine rounds of chemotherapy and spent a consecutive month in Nationwide Children's Hospital. During my battle I had a spinal tap, a surgery to insert a "port" (allowed doctors to transmit any IV medication through this and made it less painful/quicker), and a few others. I was often on many steroids, and they influenced my weight . . . It did make for the cutest pictures though. We quickly learned that laughter is the best medicine.

The most common misconception is that I wish I could forget all about my battle with leukemia. Who would want to remember a disease that took two years out of your childhood memories, right? Truth is, I only understand what my parents choose to tell me with the exception of a few unforgettable procedures. I wish my parents did not have to remember taking me to multiple doctors and watching me undergo extensive tests before that one revealed the truth. I wish that my family was not constantly worried about their three-year-old niece, granddaughter, or sister who was in the hospital missing out on major holidays. I want those memories to disappear for them. I can barely recollect anything. They are the ones who could tell you it all, every diagnosis, every test, and every procedure up to that day where the pitter-patter of little feet was interrupted by a buildup of tiny white blood cells.

What amazes me is my family's strength. We turned to our faith and church community. I think this is why we are as strong in our faith today. We know what can happen when you have faith and trust in God. Another reason we got through was because of my great-grandma. She died in 2011, but she was my angel and prayed constantly by herself and as well as with me when I would spend time with her. Not only did I stop walking at her apartment, I also learned to walk again in her apartment. She gave me strength. She gave off hope through her smile and laughter. She impacted the outcome of my entire life. She is now my feet and the legs that guide me to each destination.

> **What amazes me is my family's strength. We turned to our faith and church community. I think this is why we are as strong in our faith today.**

My grandma's apartment gives me hope and perspective every time I drive by it. It's the ultimate symbol of all the hope and happy laughs as well as tears that made that petite apartment a safe haven. Leukemia affects the lives of many families every year. For me, the effects of cancer have not intently influenced my life. I have learned to accept the actuality of the whole experience. It's not only the strength

I was given to be a survivor but my family's integrity to keep fighting with me. If only every patient had the "army" I had to support them. My family has become a substantial supporter of Nationwide Children's Hospital, and as a child we often donated Christmas gifts to be delivered to the unfortunate victims of this heartless disease. Related diseases like this impact how I think about my future. I would like to become a nurse practitioner and specialize in hematology/oncology as my doctors have made a huge influence in my life and I want to help other children in learning how to walk again.

STORY 3

Pastor Ryan Smith

I SAT IN MY car trying to catch my breath. I couldn't. My world was spinning, and I had no clue what just happened. I mean, I heard them. I was pretty sure they said I was fired and had three days to clean out my office. But that couldn't be right. I was the first youth pastor they had in the church and had been there for four years. I bought a home and started a family in this small town. I served faithfully, and I was well-liked by everyone.

I felt light-headed. I told myself to breathe. It wasn't coming voluntarily. I literally had to tell myself to breathe.

In one moment, my whole world changed, and for no reason except territorial jealousy in the church.

> **I sat in my car trying to catch my breath. I couldn't. My world was spinning, and I had no clue what just happened.**

I started the car and headed home. All I could think about was my wife and my two boys. The youngest was not even a month old yet. What would my wife think? How was she going to react? What were we going to do?

I called my parents, and they told me to come home for a few days.

A few days ended up being a few months.

Fast-forward four years, and I was practically in the same situation. We had just bought a house. Our youngest, a girl, was only a few months old. I had been the full-time youth pastor of the small-town church for four years.

Life was good. Really good.

But then cracks began to show. The senior pastor was having some medical issues. The leaders in the church were looking to give him some time off and wanted me to fill in. The pastor thought it was a coup and we were in the works of trying to remove him.

On Father's Day, a spiritual battle that physically manifested itself broke loose in the middle of the service. The pastor began to mention people by name and the different sins they had committed. Over the years he had counseled many, and he wasn't holding back. People began to squirm, and many started sweating profusely. I stood up and asked visitors to leave. The music pastor got up and jumped off the stage to punch me while his mother-in-law, the church matriarch, yelled, "Everyone for the pastor, to the stage!"

My wife and I quickly grabbed our children and fled. We never walked back into that church.

The days following were a whirlwind. People came by to pray with us and counsel us. Others drove by the house slowly and made threats.

We moved to the only place we felt safe—my parent's basement.

I was an out-of-work youth pastor, turning thirty years old, and living with my young family in the basement of parent's house. Life was hard.

And then I fell in love with the ravens.

I came across 1 Kings 17:1–7. It is the story of when Elijah had just come from a tough encounter with the king and found himself in a valley, literally.

Now Elijah the Tishbite, from Tishbe[a] in Gilead, said to Ahab, "As the Lord, the God of Israel, lives, whom I serve, there will be neither dew nor rain in the next few years except at my word."

Then the word of the Lord came to Elijah: "Leave here, turn eastward and hide

> **The power word for me in this passage is *there*. God tells him to go to the loneliest place he can imagine. No human contact of any kind. The only interaction he will have is with ravens who will feed him "there."**

in the Kerith Ravine, east of the Jordan. You will drink from the brook, and I have directed the ravens to supply you with food *there*.

So, he did what the Lord had told him. He went to the Kerith Ravine, east of the Jordan, and stayed there. The ravens brought him bread and meat in the morning and bread and meat in the evening, and he drank from the brook. (1 Kings 17:1–7 NIV, Emphasis mine.)

The power word for me in this passage is *there*. God tells him to go to the loneliest place he can imagine. No human contact of any kind. The only interaction he will have is with ravens who will feed him "there."

Elijah obeys, and God comes through on his promise. Elijah goes to where God tells him to go, and God provides everything Elijah needs by ravens.

Ravens are scavenger birds. They were considered unclean and weren't allowed to be touched or eaten. But God is using them to provide life for Elijah in Elijah's "there."

I began to realize that God has a "there" for all of us. It is a place he takes us to remind us of his provision. In this place we can recenter our faith and build our trust in God. "There" is a place we can't rely on anything else but God.

"There" for me was my parent's basement. I had no job and a wife and three small children to provide for. "There" was where I was no longer a youth pastor, where my degree didn't matter, and I had no office lined with theological books.

"There" was where God showed himself in amazing ways.

Fast-forward another twelve years. I am in the valley again.

After serving for twenty-one years as a full-time youth pastor, I am no longer in paid vocational ministry. Not because of something crazy or immoral that I have done. I am simply tired. My family is tired.

The title of *pastor* no longer applies to me. I no longer spend countless hours counseling teenagers and their families. I no longer pull crazy all-nighters during lock-ins or sit at my desk to craft a message I hope will impact the life of someone in my ministry.

> **But this I know: God continually sends his ravens, and he is faithfully providing.**

My identity has been called into question. "Who am I if I am not a pastor?" "What job options are out there for someone who has served in a church for the past twenty years?" "Are we going to have to move?"

These questions and more have flooded my mind countless times over this past year. I am starting a new chapter in my life—a chapter that is unknown to me and a little scary. But this I know: God continually sends his ravens, and he is faithfully providing.

I am eating with ravens.

STORY 4

Ashley Boreman

IT ALL STARTED when I was around twenty-three weeks pregnant in the beginning of September 2010. I was lying in bed and started to feel tingling in both of my feet and numbness in my toes. I wasn't sure at the time what was really going on, so I ignored it. A couple days later, I was at work, and I started to get the same feeling in my arms. Every time I would try to pick anything up, it hurt, but it was also hard to keep anything in my hands. My boss knew I wasn't feeling right and sent me home.

When I got home, I called the doctor's office and talked with a nurse. She claimed that the baby must be lying on a nerve and to try stretching or to lie in different positions. That night I was up all night doing everything I could think of because now my whole body felt like I was run over with a semitruck. I even tried standing on my head to try to get this baby to move.

The next day I knew something more was wrong than the baby on a nerve because I could barely move. I made it to my grandmother's house, where she could help me with my niece, nephew, and my stepson. They all had stayed at my house for the weekend. All I wanted to do was try to rest and sleep since I didn't get very much of it during the night. Later that evening I woke up and was in more pain than I have ever been in my whole life. I tried to get up and could barely walk. My grandma said, "We are going to the emergency room."

Trying to walk into the ER took everything I had to make it through the door. I couldn't understand what was going on with me. I had been so healthy and having the best pregnancy. I never had morning sickness, and baby was doing well. So what was happening to me? We waited and waited in the emergency room, and doctors gave me nothing. They said they didn't know what was wrong with me and sent me home with no answers.

Less than twelve hours later, I got up with my boyfriend Brad, my baby's father. He was getting ready for work, and I needed to go to the bathroom. I stood up, took maybe one step, and fell straight to the floor. I literally could not stand up. I didn't have any use of my legs! I was scared and mad because I was just at the hospital and they sent me home with nothing. Now there I was, helpless on the floor.

Thank goodness Brad was home and was able to carry me to the bathroom and back to bed. I had no idea what was happening to me, but what I did know was I was going back to the emergency room. This time I wasn't leaving until they figured it out and gave me answers. Brad had left for work, and my other set of grandparents came to get me and my stepson. My stepson Branden was so brave at the age of seven, telling me everything was going to be OK and it was OK if he missed school today but had to go tomorrow. Right there, in that movement, I knew I had one amazing kid because he had made all of us laugh and forget about what was going on for a few minutes.

When we got to the emergency room my grandpa carried me into the hospital. My grandma started to yell at the staff, saying, "She was here yesterday and was sent home. Now she's unable to walk, and we are not leaving until you figure out what is happening to her."

The doctor's took blood and kept trying to think of what I had. One said that I probably had MS. All I

> **In that moment I stopped and prayed for myself, hoping that these doctors were wrong and that my life wasn't about to be over.**

could do was cry and cry because I knew if that was what I had, I was dying and I was going downhill very, very fast. It was only going to be a matter of time and my life would be over. In that moment I stopped and prayed for myself, hoping that these doctors were wrong and that my life wasn't about to be over.

While we were waiting on different tests, my grandparents thought it would be a good idea to call my mom, who was living in North

Carolina at the time. They knew it would be better if she came home to Ohio. Just then it was like God blessed us all when a new doctor came in and said, "I believe I know what you have. It's called GUILLAIN-BARRÉ syndrome."

I remember me and my grandparents were like, "What in the world is that?" None of us had ever heard of such a thing. He said it is a muscle weakness caused by the immune system. He said that I would get better; it was just a matter of time. He also said even though he was 99 percent sure of the diagnosis, he had to do a spinal tap to be 100 percent sure. That's when I knew God was with me. Even though I was so scared after hearing what all the other doctors said, this doctor knew what I needed and how I needed to be treated.

A couple of weeks had gone by, and I was moving from one hospital to another. The doctors thought I was doing well until they saw my liver enzymes had spiked. This was when they sent me to another hospital. I remember the ride being so painful every bump felt like a nail poking my body, and I just couldn't wait to get there.

It seemed like every minute was an hour. My pain was starting to increase more and more. They finally figured out a medicine I could take that wouldn't be so harmful on the baby yet would help keep me comfortable.

One night they came in as I was sitting up eating and asked me to take some medicine. I remember it was a liquid. As I swallowed the medicine, I couldn't breathe. I felt like I was dying. I aspirated; this nasty virus had made its way up to my lungs. All I can remember is I blacked out. They had to put the oxygen mask over my face. When I had woken up hours later, I was hooked to all kinds of machines, and I was on a ventilator. My whole body from my face to my toes were now paralyzed, and I couldn't speak. All I could think about was, *Is my baby OK, or did I lose him while I was passed out for all those hours?*

My mom was in the room by then, and her first words to me were, "The baby is OK." I felt so relived and happy that my baby boy was OK and still hanging in there strong. Once again, I knew I had God with me watching over my son and me. It was very hard for the next couple of weeks, maybe it was even a month. I was able to understand everything that was going on around me, but I couldn't communicate. Sometimes I remember being so scared if I didn't see my mom in the room when I woke up. She was the only person who had figured out a way to talk with me. Plus, some of the nursing staff didn't know what my needs were, and some of them were even abusive. I couldn't defend myself, and all I had was the comfort of my mom.

> **All I could think about was,** *Is my baby OK or did I lose him while I was passed out for all those hours?*
>
> **My mom was in the room by then, and her first words to me were, "The baby is OK."**

It was now November. I was sitting there, and even though I was paralyzed, I could feel a sharp pain. It was contractions. This was amazing because during this whole time, I couldn't feel the baby move or anything. The only way I knew he was OK was through the ultrasounds they did, along with me being hooked up to machines that detected his heart rate.

The doctors were planning on taking the baby at thirty-four weeks because I was not getting any better and my son was literally sucking the life out of me. My son had a different plan—he was ready to join us at thirty-three weeks. I was sitting up in my bed, and I felt like I had wet myself, which wasn't possible because I had a catheter. I was amazed that I was able to detect that something was going on. I was still not able to talk or move on my own.

My mom was in the room and could tell I was trying to tell her something was wrong. When she lifted my sheet, she saw that my water had broken, and her grandson was ready to join us. The doctors all got together and took me to another room. As I looked around, there were doctors everywhere. I had over twenty people in my delivery room and ten more outside the room. Even though they had dealt with this virus before, they had never dealt with someone being pregnant with it. They weren't sure what was going to happen to me or the baby.

Well, before I knew it, it was time. He was coming whether we were ready or not. As I was lying there, my body took over to deliver this baby; and by a miracle, I was able to push. The doctors and I were all in shock that I was able to push. Even if it was only a little push, it made such a difference.

On November 19, 2010, my son Blake entered the world at 1:00 p.m. He was so tiny—four pounds, one ounce. The doctors held him to my face so that I could try to give him a kiss, but I couldn't. All I wanted was to say, "I love you" and kiss him, and I couldn't. Even though I was so happy, I was also so sad because I couldn't give my child the love that I wanted to give him. I asked God to stay with him because I couldn't.

> **On November 19, 2010, my son Blake entered the world at 1:00 p.m. He was so tiny—four pounds, one ounce.**

The doctors took him away and took me to another room where I had to stay by myself. This was the first night I had to be alone. My mom wasn't allowed to stay with me. I felt so scared and alone. The nurse who was taking care of me wanted nothing to do with me. She said it was a waste of her time to take care of someone that couldn't do anything. I remember lying there crying and asking God to please keep me safe and to get through that night. My mind was all over the place I was worried about my newborn baby, and now I was worried about what this person was going to do to me.

I didn't sleep very much. When my mom was allowed back into my room, she saw me crying, and I knew I had to tell her what had happened. My mom got out her alphabet board; it took a while to get out everything, but I did it thanks to God's strength.

After giving birth to Blake, my body was on the upside. A few days went by, and the nurse came in and wanted to try the valve in my trach. I hadn't been able to use it since the surgery because every time we would try while I was pregnant, I would instantly lose my breath. But not this time. When we stuck the valve in, I was able to say hi. It was so amazing! I was so excited that finally, after not being able to say a word for months, I could now use my voice. And my son would be able to hear me for the first time. I couldn't leave it in for very long at a time at first because it wore me out. But I knew I was on the upside of things.

As December hit, I was moved to the physical therapy side of the hospital. I was so determined to get out of there and go home. I wanted nothing more except to be able to hold my son without help or pillows. I was trying so hard to get my hands and legs to work. But those weren't the only things I had to work on. I also had to figure out how to swallow whole foods.

Christmas came, and I got my wish. I could go home but only for the day. It was amazing and such a blessing on Christmas to go home and get out of that hospital. I felt so blessed to be where I was at because it wasn't that long ago when I was like a vegetable, lying in a bed not able to do anything. This Christmas was the best and meant more to me than any other. I hated when the time came to go back, but I knew I was going to be out soon for good.

> **I know God was with us every step of the way and he gave me the most precious gift of them all: life.**

January 4, 2011, was that day. It took many months of a lot more therapy, but I knew I could never give up. I had made it through the worst, and not just me, but my son too survived! I know God was with us every step of the way, and he gave me the most precious gift of them all: life. I would work as hard as I could to live and be grateful for each day. A couple of months went by, and for the first time, I was able to hold my son, pick him up, and button his onesies by myself. Another month or so went by, and I was walking again. God never left me through this whole thing, because on the days I felt like giving up and could barely keep going, he was there for me. I thank him every day for staying with me and keeping my son and me safe. My son is a definite miracle.

STORY 5

Deon Howard

Walked Away from Sin

THE PERFECT SUNDAY had arrived, and I was prepared to present my plan of action to my pastor—the plan to dump God and the church. After all, I was living a double life and the conviction of walking on the platform once more to lead worship was irritating. I was finally ready to be liberated from the guilt of sin that plagued my mind for months of being involved in a homosexual relationship.

I approached my pastor with confidence, "I'm attracted to men; I'm leaving the church." I knew how the scene would play out—I was prepared to be criticized and beat over the head with Scripture.

My pastor had the sincerest, most compassionate smile on his face as he gazed into my eyes after my statement, and with the calmest tone of voice, he responded, "I know what you've been going through and I am not going to allow you to walk out on God because of a struggle."

> **After he finished, love consumed my very being—I had a reality check that God's purposes for my life were greater than what I was dealing with.**

I was dumbfounded by his response. Like, he didn't even address the issue at hand—he addressed my purpose in life; he addressed the call of God. After he finished, love consumed my very being—I had a reality check that God's purposes for my life were greater than what I was dealing with. I walked away with a fresh revelation of the love of God.

That crafty devil fed me lies for years and convinced me that situations in my life would always remain—he convinced me that there was no hope for freedom as it related to my sexuality. But all the while, God was screaming in my spirit . . . "Mistaken identity!" God constantly reminded me that this was a war against my identity in Christ. Earlier this year, I posted a statement on Facebook:

"Deliverance from homosexuality for me was never about becoming a heterosexual. It was about becoming a son of God." Before the foundation of the earth, God mapped out a specific plan and purpose for all of us (Ps. 139:16) and as sons and daughters of God, we have every right to inherit what is rightfully ours because of what Jesus did on the cross for us. Deliverance is our right!

If you are in a situation where the enemy is trying to pin you with an identity that doesn't line up with the Word of God, declare the truth of God over your life and refuse to accept the lies of the enemy. There is extreme danger in exchanging the truth of God for a lie (Romans 1:25), and this was the driving force behind my plan to dump God and the church. Agreement with the lies of the enemy will snuff out the voice of truth and will lead one down a dark path, but choosing to believe God and take him at his word will result in divine intervention from the lover of our soul.

Deon Howard *is extremely passionate about the plans and purposes of God and is dedicated to inspiring righteousness in the lives of people around the world. You can join the "Identity in Christ Movement" today and receive inspiration that will help you run the race in Christ and live your best life now. You can also follow Deon on Periscope @KingzKid.*

> **Friends, there is only one method: grace through faith (Ephesians 2:8). If we will simply choose to believe God and maintain an inward posture of faith (hope), the grace of God will intervene in every area of our lives, and we will walk in the victory that was ordained for us before the foundation of the world.**

(Originally published in https://www.charismamag.com/spirit/spiritual-growth/34186-what-this-pastor-told-a-homosexual-man-who-wanted-to-leave-his-church.)

STORY 6

Brittany R. Fikes

I Should Have Been Dead a Long Time Ago

IN 1997 MY family and I lived on Taylor Avenue, very close to Pilgrim Elementary School. I was six years old at the time, careless and free-spirited. I dreamed of being a huge singer someday and wanted to be friends with any- and everyone. I was blessed to have a two-parent home where the man was king of the house and my mother the queen. This was our foundation. Growing up as a minister's daughter, I never really knew what that meant back then. But it turns out, I have a family full of evangelist and ministers. Life was just pure and amazing!

Have you ever woken up and never thought in a million years you'd see your child lying on their deathbed? Well, I was that child. One distinct morning was somehow not as planned. My mom was in a rush to make sure I made it to school on time. I was running late and only had a few steps to make it across the street. It was cold; I wore my brand-new coat my parents just bought for me. I gave kisses to my mother for a warm heartfelt breakfast and grooming me for school. I heard her say, "Brittany, remember to look both ways. I'll be right here on the porch to see you walk across to school." I answered back, "Yes ma'am, I love you, Mommy!" Then, *BOOM!*

> **Then, a semitruck came speeding through the twenty-five-mile-per-hour limit. He swiped me from my feet, and I immediately flew in the air, not knowing what was going on and, more than likely, out of it.**

Life was now suddenly gone. I was just singing, telling my mother "Bye!" as I was walking across the street. I didn't think that was the last bye she would ever hear me say. Then, a semitruck came speeding through the twenty-five-mile-per-hour limit. He swiped me from my feet, and I immediately flew in the air, not knowing what was going on and, more than likely, out of it.

God's grace was certainly with me that day, although I completely died for some time. From the story told, my mother was screaming to the bedroom for my father to wake up. There I was, lying with my brain and blood everywhere in the middle of the street. The busy road became quiet with tears and disbelief. My father picked me up and prayed to wake me from the dead! And I opened my eyes!

I was rushed to children's hospital to undergo an emergency surgery on my brain and to handle the mass of blood loss and the clotting. At this point, life had been sucked out of me. I was no longer able to walk, talk, or eat on my own. All my bones were fractured, and I had to get corrective eye surgery. I had to get help to use the restroom, and I was wearing diapers. I have no clue in the world how I made it, except God saved my life.

The doctors told my parents I would be mentally and physically impaired and I would never be able to recover. However, with the blessings of God's grace and mercy,

> **My father picked me up and prayed to wake me from the dead! And I opened my eyes!**

he kept me alive and healed me physically and mentally. I am now walking, talking, and am so happy that I survived. Now my mission is to serve God and his purpose for me in this life. I continue to walk in his steps. I still can't believe I had a near-death experience and was able to at least open my eyes when my daddy prayed for me. That season of my life was very traumatic. I was in a coma for several months, with physical rehabilitation for years. But now I can rejoice and be happy. I know it was God who had kept me alive and restored my life—perhaps, to share my story.

I am now twenty-eight years old. I am in school. I am married with children. I should have been dead a long time ago. But I am so grateful to be able to do what the doctors said I could never do! Praise God!

STORY 7

Greg Massaro

WHEN I WAS working for the Wayne County Fire Department, we were called to a kitchen fire south of Dalton, Ohio. My partner and I were sent in to search for a missing child. While doing our out-search upstairs, we could not find the child. However, to our relief, the child was found at the neighbor's house.

We were then called back into the house to help with the overhaul downstairs. This is a process in which everyone is checking for hot spots in the walls and everywhere else. During the fire fight, approximately two thousand gallons of water was thrown into the kitchen to help put out the fire.

There was water literally dripping off every item in the kitchen. The ceiling and walls were dripping wet. The counters were flowing over with water. Everything was wet. As I was walking in the kitchen, observing the damage, I dead stopped in my steps, shocked at what I was looking at on the table. I saw a Bible lying open on the table. The table and everything around the table was covered with water and debris. However, the Bible was completely dry. There was no water on the Bible or its pages. There was no dirt or debris anywhere on the Bible. I stood there amazed, looking at the Bible. I was looking all around the Bible and noticed, once again, everything surrounding the Bible was wet. I don't know how long I stood there, staring in amazement. I did not touch the Bible. I just stared. After a while, I finally closed the Bible and took it out to the dad standing in the yard.

> "As iron sharpens iron, so one person sharpens another"
>
> (Proverbs 27:17 NIV)

This is a memory I cannot get out of my head. I will forever remember the dripping water all around that Bible. Yet the Bible was completely dry and had no debris or dirt. I felt God in that moment. It's a feeling I will remember forever.

> "As iron sharpens iron, so one person sharpens another" (Proverbs 27:17 NIV).

It is the jujitsu association motto (of sorts). I do my best to instill this in the kids I work with. Encouraging kids to hang around the right people is 90 percent of their battle.

STORY 8

Bishop Cor-re-don Rogers

GROWING UP, MY life was pretty normal. I played baseball, football, hung out with friends, and played video games. I did regular things that kids did in those days.

At the age of four, I had a dream. In this dream I was standing on Calvary at the crucifixion of Christ. As I stood there, I was terrified. The blood was streaming down the cross, and some of it splattered on me. At that moment, I woke up terrified and ran into my mother's bedroom screaming and crying. My mother sat up in the bed and asked what was wrong. I began to tell her about the dream that I had. My mother sat there in shock as I told her what I saw in the dream, as soon as I was done talking, she calmed me down and called a local pastor (at 3:00 a.m.). The next day, he came to our house and I told him about my dream. It was then that I began going to church.

As I got older, my interests changed and so did my friends. I began hanging out with guys who were in their twenties. School wasn't as important to me. I was hanging out late and drinking with my older friends. It was then that I was introduced to "the hustle," more commonly known as selling drugs.

The more money I made, the less I went to school. Shortly after my eighteenth birthday, I dropped out of school because it had become a burden. Being out of school, I now had more time to hustle, and drink with my friends.

As time went on, I became more involved in the street life. I was hustling and drinking every day. I honestly didn't care if I went to prison or died at that point in my life. One night I was at a party, and during a verbal back and forth, I was shot. The guy was aiming for my head, but I tilted my head back to take the final drink of beer from the can. The bullet went in, and out of my left hand. Two weeks later, I was involved in another verbal confrontation as I sat in the back seat of a car. During that incident, I was stabbed. Looking back on those incidents today, I find it twisted that being shot and stabbed gave me street credibility, and I enjoyed the respect I received from people.

> The guy was aiming for my head, but I tilted my head back to take the final drink of beer from the can. The bullet went in and out of my left hand.

Not long after those two incidents, my cousin and I went to a local apartment complex where we set up shop. At some point, I went upstairs. When I reached the top of the stairs, two little girls were standing in the hallway. I said "Hi!" and asked if they were OK. They replied, "We're hungry." They hadn't been fed; and their mother was downstairs using the drugs we had provided.

I went to the restroom and shut the door. I stood there for what seemed like an eternity. I kept hearing the little girls saying they were hungry. I removed the drugs from my pocket and flushed them down the toilet. I went downstairs and asked my cousin to ride to the grocery store with me.

We bought about $300 worth of food. We took it back to the apartment, and I told the woman to get herself cleaned up and feed her children. I never sold drugs again. I also never hung out with anyone else who sold drugs again.

After walking away from this former life, I obtained a GED. I then applied for a job with ODRC and enrolled in college at OSU, Marion branch, and later transferred to Marion Technical College. I worked in corrections for twenty-five years. In that time, I held several positions, including sargent, case manager, lieutenant, captain, and assistant investigator.

When I was younger, I was always in and out of church. My mother took me and my siblings when we were younger, and occasionally I would pop into a church as an adult.

My cousin, who worked with me at the prison and drank with me as well, invited me to a revival that was being held at the church he had recently joined. He had quit drinking and began going to church. Reluctantly, I agreed to go with him to church that night.

> As he was preaching to a packed church, he continued looking directly at me.

As the service began, a man came out and began preaching. I had never met the man; I probably wouldn't know him if he walked into my office right now. As he was preaching to a packed church, he continued looking directly at me. After a few minutes passed, he stopped immediately, looked directly at me, and said, "Do you know yet?" Of course, I turned around to see who he was talking to, he spoke again, "No son, I'm talking to you. Do you know yet?"

Now a little embarrassed, and somewhat frustrated, I replied, "Do I know what yet?" He said, "I never do this, but I need you to come up here right now." So I got up, and slowly walked to the front. Again, he asked, "Do you know yet?" Again, I replied, "Do I know what yet?" He said, "I have to pray for you."

So he began to pray, and as he put his hand on my shoulder, it felt like electricity passed through me. When he was done praying, he said, "You have a pulpit ministry." Not knowing what he was talking about and really wanting to get out of there, I quietly shook my head as if to say, "Yeah, right."

He continued, "The Lord is going to call you to preach. You have a pulpit ministry." After he had spoken those words, he let me go back to my seat. As he began preaching again, it was as if he had never stopped. I was amazed but didn't give it too much thought.

> "The Lord is going to call you to preach. You have a pulpit ministry."

After that service, I returned to life as I knew it, drinking and going to work.

A year after that church service, in August of 2002, my mother passed away. My world was turned upside down. After getting through making the funeral arrangements and getting through the funeral, I was drained. I felt like giving up. The night of the funeral, as I slept, I entered into a darkness, a thick darkness that could be felt. As I stood in the darkness, in the distance I saw a small light. It was like a pinhole coming toward me. As it got closer, it became larger until it was directly before me. It was a face, no body, just a face—my mother's face.

Then, I heard a voice saying, "The Lord wants you to prepare for spiritual leadership." And then I woke up! I was a bit shaken. I called the pastor of the church my cousin attended at 6:30 a.m. I explained to him what I saw in the dream, and he began to shout! He then reminded me of the words spoken by the bishop a year earlier. I began going to church periodically, I became a member of the church, and was there for about a year. I was still drinking and didn't really take ministry seriously, I knew about God, but I didn't know God.

So after leaving that church, I bounced around to different churches, never joining, just visiting.

Then, in 2005, I came to visit Christ Missionary Baptist Church one Sunday morning. When I arrived, one of the ushers began leading me to my seat. As she continued walking past the pews, I said, "I can just sit here on this pew." She turned and said, "I'm taking you to the pastor's office." I asked, "Why?" he replied, "Aren't you a preacher?" I laughed and assured her that I wasn't.

She appeared to be a little shocked, but she let me sit on the middle pew and she went back to her post. She is still an usher at the church. We laugh about that to this day. She always says, "When I saw you, I just saw the preacher in you."

I met the pastor of the church. I really enjoyed his preaching, and I eventually joined the church. I spent a lot of time talking to and learning from the Pastor. Before long, I began teaching adult Sunday school. The more I studied, the more interested I became. The more interested I became, the closer I came to God.

After almost two years, I felt led to tell the pastor that the Lord was calling me into ministry.

In 2009, as I was at home studying, it occurred to me that I hadn't drank a beer in close to two months. I never looked back and have not had a beer in ten years. During that time, the Pastor began my training, and for eighteen months, I studied for my ordination. In September of 2011, I was ordained and officially a clergy member at Christ Missionary Baptist Church.

In 2012 one Saturday night, I had finished the Sunday school lesson and began to pray before going to bed. As I prayed, I heard these words: "To whom much is given, much is required."

On the next morning before service, the pastor called me into his office and said, "The Lord is leading me back to Lima, Ohio. I'll be leaving in two weeks. You need to decide if you want to pastor this church. I think you're ready, but you have to know that you're ready."

At that moment, I heard those words again, "To whom much is given, much is required." It was then that I understood, and fully believed what that old preacher had told me a few years back. I could hear his words, "You have a pulpit ministry." In June of 2012, I became the pastor of Christ Missionary Baptist Church.

That same year, the Lord led me to a group of pastors. I told them the Lord had placed unity on my heart. We then began to plan our first unity service. Those services consisted of different denominations and races. Almost five hundred people attended our first unity service at the Palace Theater in Marion Ohio. We went on to hold several more unity services. Each one became more successful than the last. I continue to work and fellowship with those pastors today.

> **Only God can do what was done in my life.**

The Lord lifted my life from the pit and called me into ministry. He has since elevated me to the office of state jurisdictional bishop for Come as You Are Perfecting Churches. I am also a chaplain for the Marion City Police Department. I was instrumental in developing the MPACT initiative (Marion Police and Citizens Together), with Lt. B. J. Gruber.

As we began working together to build trust and relationships between local law enforcement and the minority community, the work we did was recognized. The chief of police (who arrested me several times in the past) was invited to a law enforcement summit hosted by then president Barack Obama, where a video of our outings and interactions was shown.

Only God can do what was done in my life. After selling drugs, having no regard for life, becoming a full-blown alcoholic as a teenager, being irresponsible as an employee and father, and living life as though God was not real—after all these horrible things—I can't help but realize that God had his hand on my life even then. He saved me from being killed when I was shot; he saved me from dying when I was stabbed. He saved me from drinking myself to death by delivering me without me knowing.

I certainly gave God no reason to save me. I gave God no reason to call me to service. At times, I asked the Lord, "What did I do for you to love me like you do?"

Through it all, I now understand that God doesn't love me because I'm good. With everything I shared with you concerning my past, I now know that God has always loved me because he is good.

I will serve my Lord and Savior Jesus Christ all the days of my life.

Bishop Cor-re-don Rogers

STORY 9

Lydia Sibbalds

I GREW UP IN a Christian household that wasn't very Christian at all. We would pray during holiday meals and would recognize how God had an impact on our days, but it didn't go much further than that. The Bible study days had come and gone. My dad refused to attend Church, and I can't remember when my mom took me for the first, or last, time. I grew up without the example of putting God first in my life. My four siblings got into trouble with friends—and the police on more than one occasion. My parents fought 24-7, and still do. My siblings refused to be good role models, and I did not have a great example when it came to a healthy marriage where God came first, your partner came second, and your kids came third. In fact, it was the exact opposite.

It was during high school when I began realizing just how far away from God I was, and how my actions were drifting me further. However, I had no one in my own family to turn to, and my boyfriend's family held even less Christian values than my own. I didn't know how to change or how to learn. This became a past thought as college was right around the corner. I was hoping for a great experience in my life where I would make lifelong friends and find a great career. Neither of these things occurred. Halfway through my first year, I realized how a college campus pushes religion away and tells you this is the time in your life where you should "experiment" and "find yourself."

> I realized how a college campus pushes religion away and tells you this is the time in your life where you should "experiment" and "find yourself."

This was something I never wanted to hear and therefore ignored. I lost my best friend because I didn't want to follow her down an even more sinful path. Being far from home didn't help either. I am a natural extrovert, but I felt terribly alone and secluded.

Then God put William in front of me. He was a peer of mine who invited me to the Navigators, a Christian ministry on campus. I felt God's pull telling me that if I wanted to change then I needed to go. I easily listened. It was because of these amazing people that I finally found a place of belonging. I was beginning to learn how to hold myself accountable for my actions and how I could think differently about myself and others. I was becoming a better version of myself, and I loved how my spirit felt lifted. This was my sanctuary on a college campus that tried to push Christianity further away from me.

It was the Navigators who showed me how powerful the Lord is. One night we participated in a small activity during worship when we were handed a thin white cloth. Markers were then passed around, and we had to write down one word we felt held us back in life. *Anger* was the word I chose. I was angry with my family for fighting with each other all the time. I was angry with Joel, but really, it was me just pushing the anger from other situations onto him. Finally, I was angry with myself. I had wanted to change my life around for the better, but always found an excuse. Row by row we walked to the front of the stage to dip our cloth into a bowl of water.

> *Anger* was washed away from the cloth, but I could feel how God washed it away from my soul.

I knew where this activity was going, but I had no idea the impact it would have on me. I had placed my hand into the bowl, making sure to take my cloth all the way to the bottom before bringing it back up. As I saw the cloth break from the water's surface, it looked pearly white once more. I remember how my lip began quivering in that moment and how my throat tightened. *Anger* was washed away from the cloth, but I could feel how God washed it away from my soul. I tried hard not to cry in front of those around me, but I remember a few tears slipped down. I had felt the first major impact of God in my life, and it was because I wanted to set a higher standard for myself.

Once the semester was over, I transferred schools to be closer to home; but unfortunately, that meant I would no longer be able to attend the Navigators. I was back to square one. I didn't feel I could turn to my family or Joel's family because nothing had changed with them. I was slowly going back to old ways of annoyance and attitude. My job as an STNA was wearing me down, and the thought of school starting up again was stressful. I never forgot the Lord, though. I spoke to him often and prayed more. I wanted to find that place again, my sanctuary filled with good people.

What I love most about God is that no matter how much I sinned in a day, or when I wouldn't ask for forgiveness, he still listened to me. It was June 2018 when I was refusing to go into Barnes & Noble with Joel, but I let him drag me along anyway. I was standing in the business section when another woman walked over and began looking at books on the opposite shelves. She had turned to me and complimented my shoes. Had it been any other time, or any other day, I would have said my thanks and awkwardly moved on to the next aisle. However, after I said "Thanks," God spoke to me. He told me that I needed to say more to her.

That same pull I had felt almost a year prior was back. That pull led me to turn and face her, and I continued to tell her where I got them. We began a full conversation with each other, and it's because of Paige, and her husband Jake, that I am the person I am today. Paige, who began as a stranger I met at a store, had become my best friend. She introduced me to a group of people who created a positive environment. This new association of people always has my best interest in mind, both personally and spiritually.

Two months later Joel and I went to Kentucky with them for the weekend, and Sunday morning we had worshipped with thousands of other Christians. I felt blessed to be in the coliseum that day, but God still had more in store for me. Not only did I make more lifelong friends that weekend, but I also heard the song "Reckless Love" by Cory Asbury for the first time. Something about that song over all the others had tugged at my heart, my inner being. I felt my throat clench and begin to burn. This time, I didn't hold the tears back and allowed myself to cry. I cried during the entire song. When I fully welcomed the Lord in, he made sure I knew he was there.

Through this experience, I knew this was where God wanted me to remain. It is my purpose to build relationships with those surrounding me and to open my heart to them. Together we will help change the lives of thousands of people. Because I told Jake and Paige about the impact of that Sunday morning and how at peace I felt, they invited me and Joel to their church. It was this couple who allowed me to share and be transparent about anything, which led to my baptism on April 7, 2019.

> **It is my purpose to build relationships with those surrounding me and to open my heart to them. Together we will help change the lives of thousands of people.**

You will always know when God is reaching out to you. It just depends on if you listen or turn away. God does not call the equipped, he equips the called. When I heard my name, I suited up and marched forward. He didn't just listen to me and give me what I wanted. He listened to me and gave me the tools to make better choices. It was because I chose to follow God and put him first in my life that I am the happiest I have been, and it is the reason my relationship with Joel is stronger. It took me twenty-one years to find my way to the Lord and to fully accept him into my heart, but I made it there. Today, Joel and I are happily married, and we are raising a household where the Lord's name comes first.

STORY 10

Anonymous

MY MOTHER WAS a runaway at fifteen years old and was introduced into drugs and prostitution. Pregnant and with no way of knowing who the father could possibly be, she was forced to give up the child (me) at sixteen. I was given to my grandparents, who couldn't afford me. I then went into the foster system but was never adopted.

I married the first boy who said "I LOVE YOU." He became abusive the moment our child was born. Beaten, broken, and deserted, I filed for a divorce. I was left to raise my child alone while working and attending college part-time.

> **I was the girl with abandonment issues, and I feared being alone forever.**

Finally, I met the man of my dreams. Someone who loved, cherished, and provided for me. I was the girl with abandonment issues, and I feared being alone forever. We were not the perfect family. Drugs and drinking had become an issue with the man who swore to always take care of us.

He had many hidden secrets even though he had come from a well-known family in a small quiet town. There were a lot of fights and arguments. I prayed to GOD for courage, wisdom, and strength. We attended church regularly, but things would happen, and seemingly instantly, we would fall from grace. What was seven years of sobriety and worshipping as a family, suddenly went to drinking, drugs, and gambling. He had spiraled out of control. We were arguing and fighting and never getting along, but we were still in love—at least I thought.

At one point, I was having major surgery and felt like I was dying. Then the worst happened. He had decided to have an affair for three months, keeping it all a secret. She was half his age and accommodating. Chasing after drugs and alcohol is what they did. They were living the party life and feeding into his lifestyle that I so despised. Still I was oblivious to it all. My once great love who cherished me wasn't so loving any more. Large amounts of money were missing, and he was disappearing more and more.

Time for him to confess. I was so taken aback, broken, and in so much shock. How could this be? This hit me at my core. He was mine! I trusted him. We had never been apart more than a few hours at a time, and now he wasn't coming home. He had gotten a hotel room for the weekend and was doing drugs and drinking. Then he asked for a divorce. What would I do? My life was turned upside down. We yelled, we cried, we didn't talk, and then suddenly, he wanted to stay. I thought, *I can't stay with him—the lies, the secrets, the missing money, the drugs, THE OTHER WOMAN. No, no, no . . .*

But I was scared to be alone again. How could I start over? I was fifty years old. I couldn't do this again. GOD HELP ME! I didn't want to live any longer. I asked my husband to help me kill myself. (I was a coward.) I didn't want to live any longer, and he said, "OK . . . God?!" What about my grandbabies? Who will love them like I do? We needed counseling, marriage counseling. There was no marriage counseling in my area. I asked everyone, and it was brought up to talk to a Christian counselor. I set out to find one. After asking several pastors, I found one. Angie is her name. She was a lifesaver who told us if we wanted our marriage to work, we would need to

> **Fear is a consuming thing. I feared as a little girl that I would never be accepted or loved. And I truly wasn't until God took that fear.**

put God first. Not ourselves, but God. We both grew up in church, but we had forgotten or we just didn't care. What I couldn't understand was how we could heal. I hurt every second. I spoke of this thing that consumed me and my life. The devil influenced both of us.

The devil was telling me I could never forgive, forget, or move forward. I lost a lot of weight. I cried all day; I could not function. My husband was still drinking and popping pills and lying and hanging with his woman.

Angie said to write it all down, everything. "Don't leave anything out. Offer it all to God, and accept he can take the pain and fear away. Trust that God can turn it back to love and feelings of joy and comfort. You might decide you need to go different ways in the end, but you might decide to make it work. See it as love and compassion."

Fear is a consuming thing. I feared as a little girl that I would never be accepted or loved. And I truly wasn't until God took that fear. I gave it all to him. I let him have my mind, heart, and soul. We joined that little church and we are very active members now. Our little grandbabies attend as well.

It has been five years. We are still together loving, worshipping, and giving God all the praise. Still knowing that at any time we could fall from grace, but as soon as we start to stumble, we get out our Bibles and pray. We ask God again to keep his shield over our thirty-year marriage and our lives. We love him and trust in him wholeheartedly. We desperately can't wait to spend time with him daily so he can guide us through each day.

> **Therefore, what God has joined together, let no one separate.**
>
> **—Mark 10:9 NIV**

AUTHOR'S NOTE

A MARRIAGE COVENANT IS powerful. The commitment to stay together through both good times and bad strengthens marriages. It also keeps families together, which in turn helps to build strong communities. It's also important to remember that children growing up without a parent is not always easy.

The importance of sticking together cannot be emphasized enough. Our spiritual enemy would love for our marriages to break apart and destroy family systems. When we are wise to the enemy's ways, we know that we are likely to be tempted in our weaknesses. As soon as we say no to temptation, we have taken a step in the right direction.

Statistics show that when couples pray together, they stay together. Being honest with one another and praying through situations help to strengthen the marriage as well as each individual soul. This is a learned behavior we teach our children.

We encourage everyone to fight through battles to save their marriage and family. There are certain circumstances where divorce is unavoidable. However, if both parties are committed to Christ and each other, it is possible to work through any issue.

Now the LORD God said, "It is not good (beneficial) for the man to be alone; I will make him a helper [one who balances him—a counterpart who is] suitable and complementary for him" (Genesis 2:18 AMP).

> **Know therefore that the LORD your God is God, the faithful God who keeps covenant and steadfast love with those who love him and keep his commandments, to a thousand generations.**
>
> **—Deuteronomy 7:9 ESV**

STORY 11

Pamela D. Brinkley

LOCKED OUT!

SEVERAL YEARS AGO, while I was taking out the trash, I, by habit, locked the door behind me as if I were leaving for an errand. LOCKED OUT? What! How shocked I was to find out I could not get back in my house. No key. No phone. Nobody inside.

I had to walk down to the project management office. I was not really feeling it, and my natural man wanted to say "Satan, the Lord rebuke you!" Y'all know how we do it! LOL! Anyway, I had been giving the Lord control over my entire life and was determined not to let worry ruin my day.

> Trust in *and* rely confidently on the Lord with all your heart and do not rely on your own insight *or* understanding. In all your ways know *and* acknowledge *and* recognize him, and he will make your paths straight *and* smooth removing obstacles that block your way. (Proverbs 3:5–6 Amplified)

> **Now the truth of the matter is that, I had rent due and did not know how it was going to be paid and really didn't want to have that discussion with the property manager.**

So without complaint, I just headed out for a nice walk. The weather was calm, and I had a good while to pray before getting there. Now, the truth of the matter is that I had rent due and did not know how it was going to be paid and really didn't want to have that discussion with the property manager. It had been a very tough season.

Here's the back story: I had completed a very long contract assignment and decided to travel for a bit as they were working out the details of another contract that was to start in the new year. I returned after a two-month hiatus and there was nothing from the company. No e-mail. No letter. No voicemail. No phone calls. Nada. I had a fifteen-year relationship with this company with an expectation to begin consulting when they ironed out their budget.

I thought this was very strange, so I went into the office, and to my surprise, they were saying they had been trying to reach me—for months! I explained that I hadn't received one message and asked which number they were calling. They showed me the number, and to my shock, it was a number from fifteen years prior! Their system did not update my new contact information! The worst part was they had given the position to someone else because I had not responded. Ugh!

So, there I was, six months later, and there was no response to the many résumés I submitted or interviews I had attended. Funds were very low. All my bills were overdue! So I definitely was apprehensive of having to have a conversation with the property manager about where I thought the rent would be coming from and when I would be paying it. All the while, I kept hearing the Lord say, "Trust me!"

I knew the basis of trusting anything is tied to my faith. What did I believe about God's faithfulness? I knew that he did not fail if he made a promise, no matter what things looked like in the natural, and that he would fulfill it. The question was, did I believe? Sometimes the cares of life seem to bombard and assault all the faith out of me. However, I was not giving up. His word is all I had. "Now faith is the substance of things hoped for, the evidence of things not seen" (Hebrews 11:1 KJV).

I began remembering all the heroes of faith that overcame incredible obstacles and proved how dependable and reliable God was. My mind began to remember the scriptures that I had read since I was a child.

1. Noah survived the flood.
2. Moses and the Children of Israel crossed the Red Sea on dry ground.
3. Abraham and Sarah conceived a child in their old age.
4. Esther was able to overthrow an evil plot against her people.
5. The widow had miracle provision.

I then remembered how I had trusted him in previous trials:

1. My daughter had been at death's door, and she was healed.
2. My life was spared in a horrible car accident.
3. My mother's kidneys were at 25 percent functionality, and she gained 80 percent back to healthy kidneys and was taken off dialysis.

So many other times, he came through for me. I had to trust that this time would be no different. I needed a financial miracle!

As I began heading to the management office, I just began to praise God because he knew the details already and the outcome. Well, as soon as I walked into the office, the property manager said in the nicest voice (she was generally *always* very grouchy!), "Hey, Pamela, come here! I need you! You know a lot about computers! Help me, please."

> **So many other times, he came through for me. I had to trust that this time would be no different. I needed a financial miracle!**

I proceeded to walk over to her desk. I sat down, and the Holy Spirit downloaded the solution she needed into my mind and understanding. She was VERY HAPPY! Did I say it was done in five minutes?

Here's the miracle: I NEVER worked with the software program that was giving her the problem. Talk about BLINDSPOT! However, I whispered a prayer and was led directly to what caused the problem. I was then shown how to repair and ensure that it didn't cause any more problems. She was elated! She had been laboring for hours!

She then said, "OK, I'll get you the key, but let's take a look at your bill." She pulled up my account, and she said that it had not been updated. She reduced my bill by $1,090! Hallelujah! She then asked me what I was doing since I was no longer working my old nine-to-five assignment. I told her I was a business management consultant for business owners, and she gave me two more orders for work she needed done. The orders paid for all the bills that were overdue and allowed me to pay those bills months in advance!

> **Most importantly he made a way in my wilderness season and proved his love for me!**

Although that was many years ago, the memory of God's faithfulness in tough situations always helps me to realize that he is totally trustworthy, altogether faithful, and certainly dependable. Without question he delivered Noah in the flood, provided safe passage for Moses and the Children of Israel, gave Abraham and Sarah the miracle of procreation in their old age, and provided provision for the widow and her sons. Most importantly he made a way in my wilderness season and proved his love for me! He loves you too! Got a trying issue? Sickness? Financial problems? Relationship concerns? Trust him.

I thought I was locked out, but really, I was LOCKED IN!

STORY 12

Tanya Hastings Blalock

GOD'S CHOICE

DURING THE SUMMER season of 1997, my husband and I became aware that we were expecting a baby. Having had two other children with no complications during pregnancy, I was confident that all would go well with this one. For the next few months however, I carried this nagging feeling that something was not quite right.

Around the third or fourth month of my pregnancy, we had our first ultrasound. The doctor noticed an excess of fluid that should not have been there and decided to keep a closer eye on things. In the meantime, I was given a dream by the Lord. The dream was very troubling to me as, and I did not understand what it meant.

> **In the meantime, I was given a dream by the Lord.**

In the dream, a baby appeared on what looked like a TV screen. I was aware that this was my baby. There were flames surrounding my baby, and I could see stairs in the background, which I thought were leading downward.

I awoke from the dream feeling very troubled. What could this mean? My husband and I discussed it with each other. Yet still had no idea of what to think about the dream. We were still fairly new Christians at the time. Prior to this, the Holy Spirit had released to us many interpretations to the numerous dreams God had previously given us. This time, there seemed to be no interpretation.

Not long after the first ultrasound, the doctor wanted to do a second one; and in doing so, he became even more concerned. He decided that I should have an amniocentesis. This is a medical procedure that checks the amniotic fluid for any birth defects. This is performed with a very long needle inserted into the uterus through the stomach. Not being very fond of needles, regardless of the size, I was full of anxiety. The thought of having such a procedure done was frightening. And he wanted to have this procedure completed within the week!

Certainly, my husband and I were bathing this situation in prayer, bathing . . . literally! I had always prayed throughout the day since the beginning of my walk with the Lord. However, my best and most private prayer times were in the mornings during my bath. I guess you could say the bathroom was my prayer closet.

So on this particular Saturday morning, a few days before the amniocentesis was to be performed, I was leaning very hard into the Lord with prayer for my baby. I acknowledged to God that this was his child and that his will be done, even if it meant he wanted to take this baby from my husband and me. Having released all to God, he took our baby! I can't explain to you how I knew this, but I knew that our baby's spirit passed from my body into eternity. At that moment, I began to receive some of the interpretation of the prior dream that I had. The peace that passes all understanding enveloped me.

A few days later, my husband and I went to our appointment for the amniocentesis. Convinced that our baby had already passed on into eternity, we shared with the doctor what we believed and asked him if he would please perform another ultrasound first. The doctor agreed and the ultrasound showed that our conclusion was indeed correct. There was no heartbeat or movement, and the doctor confirmed that our baby's life had expired.

> **On the other hand, we were full of amazement that God would reveal his intentions to us through the dream that had been given to me a few weeks prior.**

My husband and I left the appointment with very mixed emotions. On the one hand, we were very sad at this news. On the other hand, we were full of amazement that God would reveal his intentions to us through the dream that had been given to me a few weeks prior. The interpretation of that dream came full circle after receiving the news that our baby had indeed passed.

As I stated at the beginning, this dream had been very troubling to me. But as the Holy Spirit released the interpretation, we came to realize that God's will had been done. In the dream, I saw flames surrounding our baby. These flames, as I later came to realize, were the flames of God's glory. The stairs in the background were not leading downward as I had originally surmised, but upward . . . into heaven. Amazing! That God should speak to me, and us, in such a way. I am convinced that God was preparing us for what was to come. That Saturday morning, when I came into agreement with his will and released this child completely to him during my bath, God took our baby to be with him. I will not understand the fullness of why this came to be, but God made the choice to do so. I will not question it because I am in such awe that he revealed himself to me the way he did.

My tears of sadness turned to tears of joy, and I would not change anything about this season in our lives because God's presence throughout it all means more to me than anything else. His willingness to reveal himself and his will to us is amazing! What should have been a time of great mourning, to me, was a time of great praise to our God and Father in heaven!

STORY 13

Bishop Dr. Gregory Draper

How Prayer Guided My Life

GROWING UP AS a young boy in the projects, I always realized there was something special about my family and that God's hands of love were upon us. There were twelve of us, including my parents, my nine siblings, and me. We were raised in a loving and caring home. My mother was a praying and spiritual woman who raised us to love the Lord with all our heart and mind. She worked, supported my father, and cared for all ten of her children. Beyond that, she took us to church every Sunday morning. The ten of us children would pile in the back of the station wagon on Sunday morning to go to church. My mother believed in persistent prayer, the power of prayer, and the promise of prayer; and she instilled that in all of us.

I watched my life change throughout the years. I watched people I grew up with become incarcerated and murdered. These were people I called my friends. I believe the reason I am here, living a life that represents our Lord and Savior Jesus Christ, is because my mother prayed for me and her prayers were persistent. Persistent prayer has directed my life and put a hedge of protection around me for dangers seen and unseen.

Later in my adult life, I encountered a painful journey. Within a few years' time, I lost my loving mother, my father, and most recently my sister. I've always had my mother's

> **My mother believed in persistent prayer, the power of prayer, and the promise of prayer; and she instilled that in all of us.**

guidance and was now faced with trying to figure out how to get through the difficult times alone. It wasn't long when I realized I must journey through the valley of grief, despair, and pathos. This was a turning point in my life.

I had to accept, even though my heart was sad, God said in his Word, "He [I] will never leave us [you] or forsake us [you]" (Hebrews 13:5–6 HCSB, emphasis mine). This was a very difficult time in my life; I had lost those whom I'd spent all my life with, and now their voice is silent on this side of eternity. I did only as I knew to do, lean on the Lord for guidance. The ability to communicate with God and to listen at the same time is powerful and poignant.

I've always known God, but my relationship with him became stronger. God promises to walk with us, including through "the valley of the shadow of death," Psalm 23. The reality of that is very real. He was with me. He got me through. I just had to trust him. I had to talk to him. Prayer not only sustained me during my difficult times, but it delivered me to the other side.

I recall my mother praying and asking God to open doors for all her children. As much as I tried to direct my life, the Lord led me to become a pastor, a mentor, a teacher, and a leader. I learned there were people out in the world who needed a support system like I had growing up. I prayed and the Lord put it on my heart to start an organization called Knowledge Academy Educational Services. It serves to help children and families who are less fortunate with an emphasis on education in every area. I mentor and educate cancer patients and help with veteran services. I organize a summer camp and try to instill in children just how powerful God is and how prayer changes lives. I remind all those who cross my path that it doesn't matter where you start in life, but where you end.

STORY 14

Mandy Nippert

WAIT

WHEN I WAS a little girl, the one and only dream I wanted to fulfill in life was to be a mother. I loved playing with dolls, like any other little girl my age. I liked babysitting and felt when I grew up, my job would be a teacher. I had a good childhood, except for my parents getting divorced when I was eight.

> **When I was a little girl, the one and only dream I wanted to fulfill in life was to be a mother.**

Time seemed to stand still as I waited to grow up and be a mommy. But as life would have it, I soon became a teenager, got a fast-food job, and eventually got married. We were ready to start our lives as a married couple, and since I'd married a man who wanted to father several children, we started trying to get pregnant right away.

In 2001, a year after I was married, I was diagnosed with stage 4 endometriosis and precancerous cells on my cervix. I went through various testing, procedures, and surgeries to make me healthy enough to try and reproduce although I was told my chances of getting pregnant were now limited due to my health. I started reproductive medicine and saw countless infertility specialists. We considered in vitro but because of financial hardship, decided artificial insemination was the route we needed to take instead. We tried this after several drugs (pills and intravenous) and shots. We ended up trying it twice, and neither time succeeded. In 2004, I was told by a doctor in Pennsylvania, a specialist, that I had a less than 2 percent chance of conceiving. It was recommended we quit trying. I was heartbroken to say the least. After many sleepless nights and terrible days of depression, I finally decided that the future I'd always dreamed of was not going to be attainable after all.

While driving to work one morning, I was listening to my praise and worship music trying to figure out what God's plan was for my life. I was sad, but my loving and supportive family wouldn't let me give up. I was praying. I looked up at the white pickup truck in front of me and the license plate read *WAIT*. I took that to heart. I felt the Lord was speaking to me through that Ohio license plate. It might sound silly, but God works in mysterious ways! Several days after, a friend whom I worked with brought a packet about adoption into me. She passed it on to me and spoke these words. "I thought you and John might like to take a look at this."

It was six to eight hours later, my husband and I were crying tears of humbling, sobering, and loving joy. God had spoken to us that fast. "Your son is in Guatemala." The CD she had given us was from an adoption agency in Portland, Oregon, and they worked with several different countries in international adoption. I had never considered or even knew anything about Guatemala but had a heart for Central and Latin America, and well, God knew that.

That evening, we called our parents and told them we had decided to adopt a baby boy from Guatemala. To say they were shocked would be an understatement. They were completely supportive. Thirty-seven months later, my son was born on July 19, 2007. We went on our pick-up trip to bring our son home that March.

> That evening, we called our parents and told them we had decided to adopt a baby boy from Guatemala.

When he was born, we went to Guatemala to sign some paperwork and meet with lawyers and got to stay with him for a week. We had to leave him at age three weeks for six months. I look back and wonder how

I got through that time. It was God and ONLY God. We came home empty-handed, but our heart stayed there while we waited.

That March we got a phone call. There was a very specific time frame and deadline for us to go and pick up our child: the next day! If we did not meet this time frame, we would be in grave danger of losing him. The government authority was holding our "pink slip," and if we didn't get there to sign and continue, our adoption could fail.

We called our parents, got credit card numbers, called the airport, got a flight, and packed the essentials. Without knowing what would happen—if we'd get there in time, if we had everything we needed or if anything was even going to work out—we put it all in the Lord's hands and just went. No time to question anything. I had to get to my baby, and I was NOT coming home without him.

We made it in record time. We made it to the orphanage to get my boy, we made it to the lawyer's office, and yes, the US embassy. After eight days of figuring out how to be a family of three fast, we made it back to the USA, and we were parents of a dark curly haired little boy. God promised me I'd be a mommy, and he followed through. I just had to WAIT.

Four years later, in April, I was in the hospital recovering from a ligated splenic artery aneurysm while twenty-five weeks pregnant. Yes, you read that right: pregnant. Surprise! God is bigger than any doctor. Remember that endometriosis, that stage 4 that would prevent me from conceiving? Well, in essence, it saved me and my middle child's life. At twenty-five weeks pregnant, I started having unbearable pain. Because it was the first time I'd ever been pregnant, the pains scared me, and I went to the emergency room. The pain was so intense that they thought I had ruptured my appendix.

> **God is bigger than any doctor.**

An MRI revealed I had a 1.6 mm aneurysm in my splenic artery, and it was going to burst at 2 mm. If I went into labor and pushed, my unborn son and I would probably have died. The doctors told my husband he needed to be prepared to choose which one of us to save. They told me I'd lose my spleen, and they had an incubator beside me the whole time to get ready to transport my twenty-five-week-old fetus to the local children's hospital and "hoped he would make it."

Four hours later, I woke up in the SICU with both my spleen and my unborn baby (who was still attached to my uterus). They were able to ligate my aneurysm, and the baby was fine. They saw the baby in the sac as they performed the operation, and this was something these doctors had never done before. I was a walking miracle, and so was my baby. We were famous people at the hospital that month! Talk about a humbling experience. I was kept on a very close watch for the rest of my pregnancy, and a high-risk doctor monitored every move we made. I delivered my baby via emergency c-section on July 19, 2011, my adopted son Isaiah's fifth birthday.

The next part of my story about waiting is also amazing. When I was twenty weeks pregnant, I decided to name my middle son Levi. Levi means "attached." Thank goodness he remained attached during our surgery. And thank goodness for this second miracle. All we had to do was wait.

Life up until delivery of Levi brought struggles. Normal, everyday struggles. That and big ones too. Financial problems, moving, health issues, job losses, you name it. Lots of trials. But seeing my promise Isaiah and my miracle Levi together made the last eleven years so worth it.

My story doesn't end there. In 2014, November brought totally unexpected news of a THIRD BABY. I was pregnant yet again! This pregnancy was easy-peasy! Literally no issues, but you better bet your bottom dollar I had a high-risk doctor taking care of us. God specifically told me that this baby was mine because he loves me, and he wanted to give me a gift. That gift is named Samuel. He was born that February via c-section, another perfect baby boy.

When God told me to wait, I had no idea what I was waiting for. I just heard him, I obeyed, and I waited. You never know when your moment will come!

These are photos of my three sons that I took over this past year.

STORY 15

Pearl Basinger

IT WAS A Thursday evening. I was at work at Rubbermaid in Wooster, Ohio. I received a phone call from someone saying my husband was in the ER at Orrville Dunlap Hospital. He had a heart attack, and I was told I must go at once.

I went to the hospital, and they told me my husband Doyle had a heart attack. After checking him out, they said he needed to be transferred to Canton Aultman Hospital by ambulance. He was admitted to Aultman, and the doctor there was Dr. Milan Dopirak, a super doctor. Doyle had a heart catheterization, but things were not looking well.

He was in very critical condition, and the doctor didn't give us much hope. I called our two sons, one in college at Ohio University and the other at Hocking College. They arrived at the hospital around 3:00 a.m. There wasn't much hope, as the heart attack was very severe.

At the time of the attack, Doyle was at a board meeting of our home church. Two of the ladies at the meeting were RNs and knew what was happening. They immediately called the Kidron squad to take him to the hospital. The church people began praying, as well as our families and friends.

Doyle remained at Canton, and then again, early Sunday morning I received a call from a nurse saying, "You need to come at once. He has taken a turn for the worse." My family, brothers, sisters, and their spouses, as well as Doyle's family and our pastor at the time, Elno Steiner, all came to be with me, Julie, Keith, and Mark.

They put us in a room, and we prayed. Doyle had turned blue, and they thought he was going home to heaven. However, they were able to get him stabilized and wanted to take him by helicopter to the Cleveland Clinic. The doctor on call said, "I called for the copter myself as the last time someone miscued, and the copter never came." He said, "I want to be sure this time." But God intervened, and again the copter never came.

> **But God intervened, and again the copter never came.**

We felt he would not have survived the trip to Cleveland, so that was our God at work. He was in the hospital for three weeks and survived. Every time we had a doctor visit with Doyle, they would say to us, "I never thought you would ever live the night through when you came in with the heart attack."

That was in 1989!

Two years ago, Doyle again was not feeling well. He had blood work done and a bone marrow test. The oncology doctor said he had MDS and that one day it would probably go into leukemia. He did the chemo drug Vidaza for two years, and again the doctors were amazed at his blood count numbers. I said, "That is our God at work." After the two years, the doctors stopped giving him Vidaza, and they tried a new chemo drug, but again that did not work.

God called Doyle home to heaven on March 16, 2019. We are thankful for the extra years our God had given to us. We celebrated our sixtieth wedding anniversary last August 15 with a trip to Nova Scotia and Pei. It was a beautiful trip!

STORY 16

Sha'ri D. Birchfield

IN 2002 MY husband, Newman S. Birchfield Jr., and I moved to Columbus, Ohio, from Ashland, Kentucky. We decided to move after my husband spent time in training at Liebert Corporation in Delaware, Ohio. Newman started his training in 2000, and I had a chance to go to Columbus and stay with him while in training. We stayed at the AmeriSuites the first time during his training, which is now the Hyatt Place on Dimension Drive, located on E. Campus View Boulevard. The second time I visited him in Columbus, we stayed at the Embassy Suites on Corporate Exchange Drive.

While I was visiting my husband, we would ride around the far north end of Columbus from Morse Road to Delaware, admiring the areas. We went to church with some friends, and we both fell in love with Columbus. While we were at church one Sunday morning, we both heard the Lord's voice telling us to move to Columbus. God had already revealed to us back in 1997 that we were going to move, but he did not say where. In 1997, God spoke to both me and my husband Newman at the same time. He was at work, and I was at home in the kitchen cooking. When Newman came home, he told me he had something to tell me. I told him I already knew what it was. I told him that God said we are moving—moving away from all our family and friends. Not only did God move us, he revealed to us that he wanted us to change our church affiliation. We became affiliated with a nondenominational apostolic church that believes in the five-fold ministry.

> While we were at church one Sunday morning, we both heard the Lord's voice telling us to move to Columbus.

After we moved to Columbus, we started a new chapter in our lives. I became pregnant for the second time. During my pregnancy I began to develop complications. My blood pressure was high, and it stayed very high. I also began to swell and have shortness of breath. I was still working while having all these symptoms. It felt like satan had begun to attack everything God was doing good in our lives.

One day, I passed out while at work and had to go home. That night I became very ill. I had shortness of breath and was throwing up fluid that looked like mucus. Newman took me to the hospital that night, and after all tests were done, I was diagnosed with cardiomyopathy and congestive heart failure. I was told by my doctor that he had to abort my pregnancy because I would not live through it. He said my heart was too weak to continue my pregnancy full-term, and I needed a heart transplant.

I was devastated and could not believe what was happening. I told the doctor I did not believe in abortions. The doctor told me he would give me two days to make the decision and that was pushing it. He said if I did not decide, then he would make the decision for me.

We called our family in Kentucky and our new church family in Columbus. Newman and I began to pray and believe God for a miracle. The next day, the baby died, and I did not have to agree to abort our child. Newman and I were devastated. We cried and then cried some more. Then I said, "We can try again." I was told by my doctor that I should never get pregnant again, and he was putting me on a medication for cardiomyopathy and congestive heart failure. My doctor said my heart was so weak, and the ejection fraction of my heart was so low that the pills would not work fast enough. So he put me on the list for an immediate heart transplant. He advised me to file for disability because my heart was so damaged that I would never be able to work again.

> *I was devastated and could not believe what was happening.*

Newman began to pray with the anointing of the Holy Ghost. My pastor came to visit me the next day. He gave me a prayer that he said God instructed him to write just for us in our situation. I was to pray the prayer three times a day until God told me to stop. It was a prayer for healing.

My Prayer

Heavenly Father, I (we) come to you in the name of my (our) Lord and Savior Jesus Christ.

In your word, according to *1 Peter 2:24 KJV*, I proclaim "Who his own self bare our sins in his own body on the tree, that we, being dead to sins, should live unto righteousness: by whose stripes ye were healed."

Lord, I thank you that I am healed, and I believe that you are the God that heals. I stand firmly on your word according to *Isaiah 53:5 KJV*, which tells me, "But he was wounded for our transgressions, he was bruised for our iniquities; the chastisement of our peace was upon him, and with his stripes we are healed."

Lord, you asked us a question through your word according to *James 5:14–15 KJV*: "Is any sick among you? Let him call for the elders of the church; and let them pray over him, anointing him with oil in the name of the Lord: and the prayer of faith shall save the sick, and the Lord shall raise him up; and if he have committed sins, they shall be forgiven him. I have done this, and I put my complete trust in your healing power and believe that my health will be restored."

Now, Lord, I know it is your will that I am healed, in good health, and prosperous. So I declare by the blood of Jesus Christ that I am healed, healthy, and blessed and will live and walk in the divine healing the rest of my life.

I believe in your holy word in *Jeremiah 30:17 KJV*, "For I will restore health unto thee, and I will heal thee of thy wounds, saith the Lord," and in *Exodus KJV 23:25*, "And ye shall serve the Lord your God, and he shall bless thy bread, and thy water; and I will take sickness away from the midst of thee."

And, Lord, you also tell me in *3 John 2 KJV*, "Beloved, I wish above all things that thou mayest prosper and be in health, even as thy soul prospereth."

Now, Lord, I know it is your will that I am healed, in good health, and prosperous. So I declare by the blood of Jesus Christ that I am healed, healthy, and blessed and will live and walk in the divine healing the rest of my life. In Jesus's mighty name. Amen, amen, and amen.

Newman joined me in the last two prayers of my day—one in the afternoon and one at night when he came to the hospital after work. Within a week, my heart (ejection fraction) improved three percentage points. It was at 15 percent, and then it went up to 18 percent. Then it increased to 20 percent and again to 25 percent. Eventually, while I was still in the hospital, my heart improved with a steady range of 30–35 percent. My doctor was amazed at the improvement and could not explain why it increased at that rate. He stated I was the only patient he had that had the medication work like that for a heart as weak as mine.

I was released to go home after about a month's stay in the hospital with an ejection fraction of 35 percent. Getting pregnant at forty years old caused me to develop pregnancy-induced cardiomyopathy and congestive heart failure, but GOD PERFORMED A MIRACLE. Since then, I have worked and have not filed for disability. I never did get pregnant after that because I went back to school, and Newman thought it would be better to try foster care.

THIS IS MY STORY—WHAT THE DEVIL MEANT FOR EVIL, GOD TURNED INTO A VICTORY!

STORY 17

Ashlee Wortz

LET ME START this by saying I have never been a big fan of change. I like to be in control. I like to know what's going to happen and have a routine. It's always brought me comfort, or so I thought. Then I met someone. Someone who was almost the exact opposite of myself. He was tall; I am short. He knew God, and I did not. He was an addict, and I had never touched drugs in my entire life.

During my childhood, my family believed in God, and we went to church on a fairly regular basis. I even remember going to Sunday school. But life happened. As sad as it sounds, I feel people will think of almost any excuse not to go to church. Perhaps they feel if they believe in a higher power, then they don't need to go to church to worship God. Maybe they don't even believe there is a God. I imagine some people might even fear religion or are afraid of death. Maybe they are mad at God because he let something happen at one time and it just didn't make sense to anyone. But he always has a plan. I felt this way during my early adult life, I just never gave God a chance. I never gave him the glory that he so deserves.

> I imagine some people might even fear religion or are afraid of death. Maybe they are mad at God because he let something happen at one time and it just didn't make sense to anyone.

I found myself falling for this man, and I couldn't do anything to stop the way I felt. I had never really had a serious boyfriend before. But I imagined that this is what it felt like to be wanted and to feel loved. When I first met my boyfriend, he told me he lived in a sober living house. I didn't think twice about what he said. I have never been a judgmental person and I had no reason to not trust him. He hadn't done me wrong, yet.

We spent countless nights laughing, watching movies, playing cards, and drinking. Nights that suddenly turned into mornings, and we both had to work the next day. I assumed his addiction was alcohol and it would all be OK. It's not like we were doing this every day. I thought we could stop when we wanted.

I will never forget the moment when I discovered it was more than alcohol. We were watching Ohio State play in the Cotton Bowl. I left the room to go to the kitchen. When I went back to the bedroom, he had my wallet in his hands and look startled. I had definitely come back sooner than he was expecting me. I asked him what he was doing. He told me that he needed to borrow some money. I knew now that he had an additional habit; I just did not know how ugly life was going to become.

Three months later, his addiction was out of control. Even though I was sober, I felt like my life was out of control as well, which was sickening. I was constantly worried. I didn't know what to do, mostly because I didn't even know what he was using. Questions constantly went through my head. *Why did I let him start this? How can I help? Is this my fault? Does he love me? Why is God letting the man that I love, love this habit more than me?* I started lying for him. Making up reasons why he was late or why he didn't come to dinner. We were both working full-time jobs yet were so broke that it wasn't even funny. I let him borrow money every payday. I took him to buy his drugs. I was officially an enabler.

When I was at work, all I did was constantly worry about him. Was he OK? What if he got some drugs that were stronger than the last time and he overdosed? He was home alone—what if he needed me? As an enabler, I thought it was safer for him to get drugs if I took him and stayed around while he used. Something now I absolutely know is not true. My anxiety was beginning to get out of hand. Handling the stress of a job I didn't like and the stress of his addiction was consuming my entire life. So I did what any enabler would do and walked out of my job that I had for sixteen years. The only job I had ever had my entire life.

Just like that, I didn't know who I was anymore. I was lost, depressed, and not in control of a single thing. The love I had for my boyfriend was as strong as ever though. He apologized countless times. He told me "Just one more time" more times than I would like to admit. He was also beginning to have some anger issues throughout his addiction. I was now on what felt like a never-ending emotional roller coaster, and I dislike amusement park rides with a passion!

> I was lost, depressed and not in control of a single thing.

Weekend after weekend, it was the same thing: drugs, booze, and cards. I quit drinking, thinking this would ultimately help the situation by me becoming an old fuddy-duddy. My intentions failed miserably, and now I just got extremely sensitive because he chose to continue the weekend party life while I sat alone. I couldn't even tell my mother or friends why I was so upset, so I kept it to myself.

One weekend, his brother was in town from Florida, and they wanted to go out for drinks. I said I would drive, so at least I knew he was safe. They had not seen each other in a few years, so I knew my night would be ugly. I should be a psychic because my predictions were head on. I had never seen him this bad before. My heart was broken. I couldn't go on living this lifestyle. At the same time, I knew breaking up with him was going to hurt just as bad. For some reason, I took out my phone that night and made him a video to show him the next morning (once his hangover subsided) just how inebriated he was. I was hoping this would make some sort of difference. The morning came, and I was clearly upset. He didn't know the details as to why I was so upset, but I am sure he had some sort of idea. I told him I made the video. He watched it repeatedly. He was asking questions about the night before. I held nothing back. This was the moment that he let God back into his life, 09/07/18.

He told me that he was going to stop using cocaine, alcohol, and marijuana. This was music to my ears! I knew it was going to be a difficult journey, but I was up for the challenge. I knew it was a disease. I knew he was a good person; he just made poor choices. The next

Sunday, we began going to church together, and we haven't missed a Sunday yet.

I found myself starting to pray—praying for healing not only for my boyfriend but for myself as well. Considering this was a new relationship I was forming with God, I did not know what to expect. I will be honest: I wasn't expecting much. I thought it was going to be a struggle to watch my boyfriend do this on his own. However, I was wrong. So very wrong. I have seen God mold him into a new man right before my very own eyes. He is a completely different person. I think he is getting to know himself again as well, as he was lost for many years. His parents tell me that they don't know what I did to him or how I made him change. There is no possible way that I can take the credit for a miracle that God has given us. He gets up every morning to read his Bible, he listens to Jesus Culture, and he prays. He prays for his new life, his family, and thanks God for how far he has brought him.

> *There is no possible way that I can take the credit for a miracle that God has given us.*

I myself have learned a lot about God as well. Someone who was once a stranger to me, I now feel very close to. I have learned that my boyfriend is still under construction and God isn't done with him yet. I have learned that when you feel you have lost control, God has never lost control, and he knows what he is doing. I am still very much growing in my faith. I am still learning every day. We have come so far, and he has carried us the entire way. Life got too hard to stand, so we both kneeled, and we are stronger than ever now.

STORY 18

David Schuster

IT ALL BEGAN on October 13, 2002. It was one week before the birth of my fourth child and second son Caleb in Nashville, Tennessee. My parents were visiting in preparation for the birth. Thankfully my mom is an RN. I suddenly fell to the floor, and it felt like an elephant was sitting on my chest. I couldn't move. My mom took my pulse, and it was extremely low. They called an ambulance who gave me nitroglycerin when they arrived because they were convinced I was having a heart attack.

After arriving at the hospital, the doctors were mystified. They kept me for multiple days but couldn't find any evidence I had a heart attack. My EKGs were normal, and no heart damage was found from a cardiac catheterization (putting a long thin tube through an artery in my leg/groin area).

> *After arriving at the hospital, the doctors were mystified.*

Before they released me, the cardiologists determined it might have been a stroke. However, they said it was too late to confirm through a CAT scan and referred me to a neurologist. The neurologist immediately identified stroke damage to my body. My left arm was extremely weak, I had trouble lifting items, and my balance was gone. When I tried to walk, heel to toe, I would fall over. The doctor sent me to PT. My memory also seemed to be swiss cheese. I remember going to one doctor's appointment and, when I came out, not knowing if I drove or if some drove me. I felt keys in my pocket and realized I must have drove, but I had no idea what type of vehicle or color. I had to set off the alarm to identify the vehicle I drove in.

During this time, my church was not there for my family. I had stopped attending due to the health event, but no one called or visited to see why. I felt led to find a new church. As I was driving home from work one evening, God led me to a church I had never been to, a Westside Cumberland Presbyterian Church (regretfully, it no longer exists). This was a denomination I had never heard of before. I began attending. It was a small church with the average age around seventy. God told me not look at the numbers or age but at their strong faith and commitment to the Lord.

I appeared to get better and, over some time, was released from PT but continued to have strange events occur. I would be walking down a sidewalk, and my left leg would give out like it wasn't there anymore. Once I was crossing a street in Nashville and fell in the road. I quickly rolled so I wouldn't be hit by a car, damaging my suit. The neurologists could not determine what was causing this. I played softball for many years and was on the softball team for the agency I worked for. In the fall of 2005, I was playing second base and a ball was hit toward me. When I went to field the grounder, I got extremely dizzy and fell to the ground. My team helped me up, and I made an excuse that I had lost my balance. Soon after I began to have events (mini-strokes) that would cause me to collapse on the ground. Sometimes my heart rate would go over two hundred, and other times it would drop below thirty. The neurologists and cardiologists had no idea what was happening, but they took away my driver's license due to the risk of this happening to me while driving. Thankfully, fellow believers pitched in; one of them drove me to work every day. Elderly neighbors drove me to church on Sundays and to Bible studies and prayer meetings.

In March of 2006, I had what is called a catastrophic health event. While walking up the stairs at work, I started to get short of breath, and my left arm became numb. I made it to my office and called for one of my coworkers who was a doctor. He came

> **While in the hospital, my heart rate would spike and then drop to below 30. The doctors told me there was nothing they could do for me and that one of these spikes would ultimately kill me.**

YOUR MOMENT IS NOW

in and saw me and immediately called an ambulance. Before I could make it to a chair I collapsed to the floor. It was hard on me to have an ambulance take me from my workplace. I was a spectacle for everyone to watch. Many people were aware I was no longer driving and were already concerned for my health.

The news was not good. At the hospital, they tried to have me take a stress test, but when I got on the treadmill, my heart rate began to spike and reached 218. The nurses panicked and got me off the treadmill and ran to get a shot to reduce my heart rate. They tried multiple things before my heart rate finally began to go down. While in the hospital, my heart rate would spike and then drop to below 30. The doctors told me there was nothing they could do for me and that one of these spikes would ultimately kill me. They told me to get my affairs in order.

We were not ready to give up, so we went through the process for me to be seen by the Mayo Clinic. We went through the process of submitting all my medical records and notes from the doctors and waited for the letter of hope saying they would treat me. Instead, less than a month later, we received a letter from the Mayo Clinic. They stated they had reviewed my records, and there was nothing they could do for me. From that time on, we began to prepare for my death.

Because I was a public servant in an appointed position, I resigned from my position. I realize now that this was very foolish. I didn't want to create bad press, but by resigning, I lost my long-term disability and life insurance. When facing death, sometimes you forget the basic things your family will need.

My wife and I began to make farewell videos for each of my children. I figured the youngest ones were too little and wouldn't remember me, so I wanted to make a video for each of them telling them why they were special and how much I loved them. This was extremely difficult. We began to make plans for the funeral and obituary notice.

> My wife and I began to make farewell videos for each of my children.

I called my good friend Pastor Michael Cousin and asked him if he would lead my funeral service. It was a very difficult call for both of us, but he agreed to do it. We picked out the cemetery. It was on Highway 100 south of Nashville, Tennessee, where I attended Easter sunrise services with my good friend Roland. I began to call a few friends whom I wanted to speak at my funeral and asked them while also saying goodbye. It was incredibly difficult, so I wrote a list for my wife for her to reach out to people after I died. Again, I wasn't being very aware of how hard this was on her.

My wife recently found my list/note for the funeral, and it is very difficult for me to read it; tears come to my eyes. How painful it must have been for my wife to read it and help me with it. The note is below; however, I have removed some last names out of respect for the people.

Cemetery—Pretty one on HWY 100, that I go to Easter sunrise services.

Speakers—Rev. Michael Cousin (minister, leading service)

- Roland (let him speak if he is led to, not mandatory)
- David P (read my reflections paper at service, add to it if wants to at the beginning or end, he always makes people laugh, this will help lighten the mood.)
- Other speakers allowed to speak if they ask
    - Rock
    - Greg
    - Rich D.
    - Mary L.
    - Meshia
    - Lisa P.
    - Mom, Denise, Donna
    - Esther
    - Jeff P.
    - Dave M.
    - Mark or Ginger
    - Carmen (if you can find him)
    - Roosevelt
    - Stephanie M.
    - Mischi
    - Hedy
    - Manny

- Why I chose people, not sure—I just want close friends or those focused on God.
- Mindy, feel free to speak if you want, but it is going to be hard enough on you just to handle the kids and sit through this, you will need Jovan & Jennifer to help you.

    I love you—trust your feelings, I trust you.

    Let Michael, Mom, Roosevelt, Rock, or someone else proclaim my faith, please!

    Thanks! You're the best.

    Remember, I am perfectly fine with you getting married as soon as you find someone who will be a good dad and will have the same goal as me (to make you happy).

    God is awesome, and he knows best. If I am no longer with you, then he has a reason, and I trust him.

Love always,
David

At times my wife was angry, but I didn't know why, because I was the one who was dying. She recommended I get counseling, which I had always felt uncomfortable with. However, I did it for her. I was concerned about getting advice from someone who wasn't God-focused, so I looked on the Focus on the Family website and found local Christian counselors. I found a Dr. Godwin and called him for appointment. How could I go wrong with a doctor with *God* and *win* in their name?

> **At times my wife was angry, but I didn't know why, because I was the one who was dying.**

I met with Dr. Godwin, and he explained that she (my wife) was going through the stages of grief, with anger being one of them. He also pointed out that she would be left alone with four small children, so she was probably angry about that as well. I went to Dr. Godwin regularly, and he told me he rarely met someone who had gotten a terminal diagnosis and yet was as content as me. I had never been truly afraid of death since I gave my life to the Lord when I was ten. I trusted in God and that I would go to heaven and have peace. However, as time went on, I got worse, and I became profoundly weak.

Two events come to mind that I can't forget.

We had a family friend come over to see me, but I looked horrible and could barely stand up. I looked like death was upon me, and it scared her. She quickly made an excuse about forgetting something important and left quickly. I truly believe she ran out because she faced her own mortality.

The second event was much worse. As I said, I have never been afraid of death, but one day I was in the family room with my little daughter Hannah, and I could feel my life slipping away. I prayed to God, begged him, to please not let me die in front of the kids. I continually prayed for God's will to be done, but I couldn't handle the thought of my little kids watching me die. Soon after, God reminded me of a verse—I don't remember if it was during my normal Bible reading in the morning or if I was led specifically to the verse. For many years I have read one chapter in the Hebrew Bible (Old Testament) and one chapter in the New Testament each morning. At the time I was primarily reading from the New International Version.

As I read James 5:14–16, my first thought was why hadn't anyone called and offered this to me? Why hadn't any of my pastor friends recommended this verse? How did I forget this verse? I am so thankful God led me to it on that day because it saved and transformed my life.

James 5:14–16 NIV says this:

> Is anyone among you sick? Let them call the elders of the church to pray over them and anoint them with oil in the name of the Lord. And the prayer offered in faith will make the sick person well; the Lord will raise them up. If they have sinned, they will be forgiven. Therefore, confess your sins to each other and pray for each other so that you may be healed. The prayer of a righteous person is powerful and effective.

I thanked God and immediately called my pastor from that little church God sent me to where the average age was about seventy. Pastor Duke's response started with an apology for not offering to do that for me but ended with praise for God. He gathered the elders together and had someone pick me up and bring me to church. Pastor Duke and the elders (Edgar, Bill, Andy, and others whose names I have forgotten) laid hands on me, anointed me with oil, and prayed for my healing in the name of Jesus! I was so thankful. Unlike others, I didn't feel an immediate result, but I truly believed this is what God wanted done, and he would use it to glorify himself.

Over the next few days and weeks, I began getting stronger. I regained my balance and ability to pick up items with my left hand. Prior to this, I needed to hold on to walls, railings, chairs to stand without swaying. If I closed my eyes, my balance had been so bad that I would fall over. Now I could close my eyes and walk. God is truly amazing, and his word is true!

> **Unlike others, I didn't feel an immediate result, but I truly believed this is what God wanted done, and he would use it to glorify himself.**

What a simple solution, to turn to the word of God and trust and obey what it said. I had gone to the experts of the world, Vanderbilt Medical Center, Mayo Clinic, and no one could help. But our God is faithful, and he is more than able. Within a few months, I was back at work at a new job. Not too long after that, I was playing sports with my kids and tennis and softball with my friends.

Our little church became known as the miracle church for a short time. People came just to see me in person. People came to be prayed over by the pastor and the elders.

I was blessed with the opportunity to preach at Pastor Cousins' church in Nashville, Tennessee, a few years ago. Regretfully the tape didn't work that day, but I trust God had a reason for that as well. I remember starting out with, not too many years ago, calling Pastor Cousins to preach my funeral and now, after being healed, having the honor of preaching from his pulpit. Many friends and colleagues came to hear me and rejoiced at the miracle God had done!

To this day, others continue to wait for me to die! They don't believe I was healed by the elders praying over me and anointing me with oil in the name of Jesus. It has been *thirteen years* since the event in March of 2006, and I am accomplishing much for the Lord in hopes of glorifying him in all that I do. I appreciate the little things: daffodils blooming, leaves on trees, and the birds chirping. I am amazed by God's creation on a daily basis and appreciate it in a way I couldn't before. My hope is to glorify God in all that I do with each extra breath that I have been given and to make my wife happy!

> **To this day, others continue to wait for me to die! They don't believe I was healed by the elders praying over me and anointing me with oil in the name of Jesus.**

As I was writing this, God reminded me of the following scripture: "Unless Your law had been my delight, I would have perished in my affliction. I will never forget Your precepts, For by them You have given me life. I am Yours, save me; For I have sought your precepts" (Psalm 119:92–94 NKJV).

STORY 19

Johnson (John) Noel

I GREW UP IN a Christian family. My parents have always encouraged us to go to church, Sunday school, and Bible study. Growing up, I was a member of the children's choir, and later I joined the men's choir. My mother always told me that church should be an important part of my life. She said I should always have faith in God and know that nothing is impossible for him. Throughout my life, Hebrews chapter 11—the faith chapter, as I called it—has been a great part of my life. I have memorized it in my native language of French as well as in English. Whenever I feel my faith is a little weak, that chapter is what I run to for comfort.

After I completed my undergraduate degree in the US, I was not sure where the Lord wanted me to go and what he wanted me to do. I did not ask him for guidance or anything like that, but I decided on my own to apply for a doctorate in chiropractic medicine. I was doing everything according to what I wanted, but not what the Lord wanted me to do.

Halfway through the program, I had to stop. Soon after, I was really sick and hospitalized with pneumonia. I spent days in the hospital, but the Lord, in his compassion and his kindness, saved my life. I was mad and bitter, constantly asking why things turned out that way. I was among the top of my class but still decided to leave. It took me awhile to get back on track with my faith, to accept God's will, and to trust him fully again. God never fails us, and he never failed me. He opened

> **What I have learned from what I went through is that God wants us to include him in our daily activities.**

doors for me that I thought were not possible, and he is still working marvelously in my life.

What I have learned from what I went through is that God wants us to include him in our daily activities. He wants to be a part of our lives when things are good and when things are bad. In Hebrews 11:6 (King James Version), the scripture of the Lord says, "But without faith it is impossible to please him: for he that cometh to God must believe that he is, and that he is a rewarder of them that diligently seek him."

I would hope that everyone could try to get a little bit closer to God and always ask him for his guidance.

May God be with you always,
JOHN

STORY 20

Don Johnson

AS I BEGIN my testimony, I would like to start by saying, faith and belief in God have always been in my life for as far back as I can remember. As a family, we went to church, and I attended Sunday school on a regular basis for the first few years of my life. We always prayed at meals and before bed. My father would sing "Jesus Loves Me" to my brother and me constantly. However, most of this stopped pretty much after I turned seven years old—at least, that is what I remember.

We moved a few times and never got back into the church and my faith pretty much went to wayside. Still, prayers were said at every meal and before bedtime, but there was no church. There was no other form of faith instilled or really pushed by our family. All throughout middle and high school, I attended church off and on with friends' families. When I was asked which church my family was a member of, I told them, "None." I rarely was asked to attend church with my friends in some of these religions.

I did not understand this, as I thought church was a bringing together of all people regardless of which Christian religion we were. I lost my faith almost completely after high school. I soon enlisted in the military after my high school graduation. This was due to my behavior, in that I was not ready for even community college because of my bad attitude and poor choices throughout high school. I enlisted in the United States Army as a combat medical specialist.

> **I lost my faith almost completely after high school.**

I married my sort of sweetheart from high school, as we attended different schools. Nonetheless, I married a very staunch Catholic woman of Cuban ethnicity. Their faith and beliefs were very strong, but we never went to a Catholic church. We vowed to raise our children the Catholic way. We seemed to only go to church for the portion of Catholicism that mattered for the kids' portion. But we did not attend regular Sundays or Wednesdays at church. There was no Bible study, and more than anything, no family prayers took place. I was soon deployed for nine months out of the year, and I prayed daily and had my Bible with me in Iraq. I often asked God and Jesus for love and support for my wife and two small children.

I would call out to Jesus, asking him to spare my life and that we would all get home to our families safely. I also prayed for my brothers and sisters in the military, especially in my unit. I prayed they would all make it home alive and back to their loved ones. I felt like my faith had renewed itself and was getting stronger and stronger every day I was away.

However, I couldn't understand what it all meant and why Jesus wouldn't answer my prayers when I would go to a burning military vehicle only to pull a soldier out of that vehicle that was on fire and damaged. Why did only half of his body come out and there was no saving him? Why would God allow this to happen? Did this soldier have a family? Did he have children? What about his wife or girlfriend or mother, father, brothers, and sisters? *Why God? I asked you to protect us, and you have failed me and failed them! Why, GOD?*

> *Why would God allow this to happen? Did this soldier have a family? Did he have children?*

I had lost my faith again, or so I thought I had.

We returned from Iraq, and I was able to see my family and my beautiful children. But I did not know who I was or who my wife was. I had lost my faith in the family and in the belief that all things can change for the better through the mercy of God and believing in the positive. Our marriage ended after four and a half years. There was no church and no belief in my mind that could change who I was becoming. I was lost and only cared about becoming a better soldier, my rank, making money, and making it happen in the military.

After nine and a half years, I decided to get out of the army and move back home to Florida to see my kids and my mother and father. My brother and I were on the news as returning veterans, and all our friends were so happy for us to be able to return safely. However, they did not know or realize the pain, grief, and uncertainty we had felt and gone through. War is not pretty. Many lives have been lost. Wounds cut deep and, sometimes, never really heal at all. The pain still haunts me today as random thoughts cross my mind at any given time, and I can't shake them. The tears that fall and the pain I feel for those lost, for those I could not save or help back to health, will haunt me forever.

A few years later I met another Catholic woman. Over ten years, I enjoyed some great times, but also had some bad times as well as times of uncertainty. I prayed again that my faith would be renewed, but there was never any consistency of going to church, beliefs, and prayers. She did not like the hypocritical attitude of the Catholics. So we did not go to church unless it was for her parents and for our new son that was born. Once again, we vowed to raise him Catholic, and we did. We again went through all the Catholic ceremonies and things that had to be done under that religion. After eleven years, the marriage dissolved, and we went our separate ways. Once again, that small piece of hope that I would regain in my faith had been lost, and I strayed again.

Working has always been to better my career and myself, so I could become a better person. Again, I yelled out to God and asked him, "What is it that you want me to do? What is it I am doing wrong? I just do not get it, God. Please help me discover what it is you need." I heard and saw nothing, so I went about my life. I struggled in many areas of my life. Financially, career-wise, family distance, I was a loner that would find trouble and create horrible situations for myself, and I just did not care any longer.

After a few years, my friends pulled me back into the real world. My job was going great, and it seemed as though my life was taking a

> **Again, I yelled out to God and asked Him, "What is it that you want me to do? What is it I am doing wrong? I just do not get it, God. Please help me discover what it is you need."**

small turn for the better. I was feeling better. I was praying again. I was surrounding myself with good-hearted people, but there was something missing: CHURCH!

I met some friends who asked me to come to a dinner as they wanted to introduce me to a woman and a great friend of theirs. She was a God-fearing woman and someone they felt would be good for me and the kids. Long story short, it went well. We began to discuss religion and beliefs and what we both wanted out of church. This was very uncomfortable for me as I did not know where to begin with this kind of conversation.

She was raised very Southern old-school Baptist, and me . . . well, there was Methodist, Lutheran, Catholic, and exposure to about four other religions. I felt I was very well versed in religions and what God and Jesus wanted out of our lives, but not mine. I was as lost as ever and broken still on the inside. I was asked to attend church with this woman and friends. I quickly said I would never attend a Southern Baptist church and have them tell me I would go to HELL if I didn't follow their ways. This woman quickly stated, "What makes you think I go to that type of church?" I was raised that way but do not like that thought process either, and what was to take place next changed my life—or so I thought.

This is when my faith took a turn that I never expected at all. I was introduced to NorthStar Church in Kennesaw, Georgia, and Pastor Mike Lynch. When I heard him preach, I was moved and felt like God was talking directly to me that Sunday morning in 2004.

So we started attending regularly. I got involved in small groups, began teaching fifth grade young men who were preparing for sixth grade and prayed regularly again. Life was going be wonderful. This woman and I spent the next nine years off and on in the relationship that quickly became very toxic. Between our combined five children and her health issues, we grew apart faster than we could control. There was no life outside of the house, and I tried to grasp ahold of what was happening but couldn't.

We had separate lives for five out of the nine years we were together. There was no infidelity or abuse. There was neither a like nor love, but therein began the loss of faith again. We rarely attended church anymore. The kids were doing whatever they wanted, and the more I tried to create a balance and routine, the more I was told to leave the kids alone, as I was not their father. They were increasingly disliking me. I became very distant, and . . . I will never forget the day that I was accused of doing something horrible to one of the children and asked to move out of the house immediately or the police would be called.

I packed as much as I could fit into my car and drove to the house of a friend of mine. Again, I asked God for a reason this was happening to me. What could have been said to make this situation happen? NOTHING but silence. I was working. I was back in church. I was praying. I was attending church and teaching children how to be more GOD like. What was going on? This was in 2011.

This will be the hardest portion of my testimony. I was arrested and placed in a holding cell for seven hours. I was questioned repeatedly about an accusation made by one of children from this woman. I left scared and unsure of what just took place. I was told to not leave the state and be ready to be questioned on a short notice. I moved into a house shortly after leaving my home of ten years. I was living in a room, working two jobs, saving money and being checked on regularly to see where I was and where I was working over the next three years. I had a lawyer and there was a court date set.

My faith had been set aside because of the uncertainty and questions in my mind. Why did I not lean on GOD or ask in prayer what to do? I don't know but, I found myself praying off and on closer to the court date. I had been praying more and more and more plus attending North Point Church in the town where I had moved. But was it enough? What was I to expect in a few short weeks? I really thought my life had ended and I was going to be placed in Jail for something I would never think about doing. "Why GOD?"

> **My faith had been set aside because of the uncertainty and questions in my mind.**

Moving forward to March 18, 2014, I began dating my beautiful Sally. That is a whole different testimony, but it was her support as well as my renewed faith in church, prayer, and the true meaning of GOD and how Jesus works in our lives that gave me strength. It was the support of the Cascade Hills Church family, along with Pastor Bill Purvis and Pastor Brent Purvis who were true blessings to us.

Five months later, on August 18, 2014, three days before the court date, I received a phone call from my lawyer. I will never forget these words as long as I live. "Are you sitting down? You need to be sitting down." As I replied with a "YES!" and said a small prayer, I heard the following: "It's over, Donald. They have dropped ALL charges, as the child in question stated she was lying about the whole thing and she just did not like you in the house making rules. She had lied about the whole situation and just didn't like you."

I fell to my knees and began crying and asked at least three to five times if this was really happening and if what I had heard was really the truth. I did not feel like I knew what truth and faith really meant anymore, but I had prayed that God would guide me or send me a message somehow. My lawyer said it again, "It's over, Donald, and I hope and pray you have or can get back to some sort of normalcy in life without this lie being held over your head." I thanked him and all the detectives and police involved in the full investigation into this accusation and hoped they never had to be involved in something like this ever again in their lives.

I picked up the phone and called my sweet, beautiful Sally crying. I told her what had happened. I remember her telling me these words, "I have always felt in my heart you were telling the truth. I always believed you were a great man and a God-fearing man, and that God would show you the way and get you and us through this. I love you and I believe in you, Don." From that day forward my faith has been renewed with the help of my pastors Mike Lynch, Andy Stanley, and Bill Purvis. They have created new life in my heart, and I owe it all to Jesus Christ, my Lord and Savior.

This is Pastor Mike Lynch's Prayer that I pray daily:

Dear Jesus,

    I know you lived for me, I know you died for me, and I know you rose again just for me. Come into my heart and be my one and only personal Lord and Savior. I say this prayer in your name, Jesus, amen.

STORY 21

Antoinette Roberts

Mended Heart

I STARTED PRAYING ABOUT writing my testimony to share. As I prayed, I asked God to do two things. First, "Lord, let it bring glory to you." Second, "I hope and pray someone can be helped and saved along the way."

As I started writing my testimony, it became six long pages. I read it many times throughout the day, but something happened. As I read it, God convicted me about a person I really haven't forgiven. Writing those pages was meant for a greater purpose. I had to stop for a few minutes to recall and correct my actions. Now the six pages God had given me became a poem in a short and a creative way to share my testimony.

> I asked God to do two things. First, "Lord, let it bring glory to you." Second, "I hope and pray someone can be helped and saved along the way."

My childhood left me emotionally, verbally, and mentally scarred.
It left me thinking so low of myself.
It left me with fear, anxiety, discouragement, and despair.
Not only from my family but people unaware.

Looking in the mirror, what did I see?
No dreams for this girl it will not be.

No way of escape as the storm surge rise
I'm being tossed like a tornado high in the sky.

I started dating this young man after high school.
I thought it was love, but I was only a fool.
I know what it's like to be wanted or not.
I know this is not of God, so I asked him to untie the knot.

Hey, young lady, you are worth the wait.
Be careful and mindful don't you take that bait.
I asked Jesus, "When you send someone in my life, let it be a man after your own heart."
As the months went rolling by, my prayers were being answered part by part.

Then came one invitation to a Bible study class.
I never encountered the Lord like I had.
The preacher talked about Jesus Christ and him dying on the cross for my sins.
How much he can mend the heart and my life can begin again.

As I visit the church's Bible study every Wednesday for a few months.
I started walking closer to God and realizing all he had done.
Just for me! Just for me! I kept saying to myself.
The tears started rolling, for this love I had never felt.

I'm a sinner saved by his grace.
I've been forgiven and set free that's what the Bible says.
The more I study the word from his holy book.
Yes, it's called the Bible, for now I am hooked.

He's drawing me closer and even getting rid of some fears.
I talk to him like my closest friend is near.
Something is happening a new change has come.
My life is now brighter, as bright as the sun.

LU ANN TOPOVSKI

I thirst and thirst for more each day.
Drawing close to my Savior and his amazing grace.
He's knocking on my door, there's nothing else I can say.
But to give my life to Jesus and let him have his way.

One Friday night at revival in Louisiana,
The message touched my heart as the music played softly on the piano.
I remembered the altar call, "Come to Jesus, come to Jesus."
I knew I had to make this choice for so many reasons.

With heaviness gripping my body, it was failing, and I was falling apart.
I was in a spiritual battle, and I had to fight hard to depart.
I felt like someone was sitting on top of me, holding me back.
But I knew it was the enemy trying to steal and attack.

Finally, I walked up to acknowledge Jesus Christ as my Savior and Lord.
The enemy didn't have his way, God gave me favor from above.
A few weeks later was my baptismal day.
I fell to my knees, "For God's will," I prayed.

Something special happened as I left out the door.
God had confirmed his love for me as he done many times before.
I stepped back in the house to answer the phone.
The news came from out of state that my nephew had just been born.

Three weeks early, new, tiny, and so precious is he.
Two new births on my special day, it would be.
I felt God's love and grace overflowing in my heart.
Today is the day I will get a brand-new start.

It's my Father's love who keeps me going day by day.
I will trust and believe him as I travel along my way.

No matter where I am on this journey called life.
There will always be challenges and even more strife.

He has given me the Holy Spirit who empowers, convicts, guides, and comforts me.
No, I'm not perfect, and I will never claim to be.
But now I know that I am never alone.
What a difference it makes, to know my Father sits high on his throne.

Looking in the mirror, what do I see?
A God-fearing woman, "Yes, that's me!"
A way of escape has been provided there's no need for a key.
I'm always in my Savior's arms, and no one can snatch me.

He [God] heals the brokenhearted and binds up their [my] wounds.
—Psalm 147:3 NIV (Emphasis mine.)

Trust in the Lord with all thine heart; and lean not unto thine own understanding. In all thy ways acknowledge him, and he shall direct thy paths.
—Proverbs 3:5–6 KJV

Written by Antoinette Roberts

STORY 22

Meredith Hancock (✝)

OVER THE PAST twenty years, I have been faced with a lot of struggles in my life. My faith in God has been challenged in so many times, it's become hard to keep count of them. Over that time, I have had seventeen surgeries and lost twenty-three close friends and family (including my brother at the age of forty-three and a half-brother at forty-two) to various cancers, suicide, and drug overdoses.

I have moved my home six times while trying to figure out where I belonged after a divorce. I have been hospitalized multiple times and broken several bones. I moved from Maryland to North Carolina because I had a broken kneecap and did not have a job. I had no money, so my mom was able to help me during that trying season in my life. In doing that, I had to leave my kids with their dad because I did not think it was fair to uproot and drag them from a place in which they always called home.

> **There are so many different stories I could tell that helped me keep my faith and get closer to God.**

Once a month I'd drive to Richmond, Virginia, after work on a Friday so I could visit with my kids for a short weekend, then I'd drive back to Richmond on a Sunday to return them to their dad. I had them on various holidays, as well as spring and summer breaks. I thank God for FaceTime. I was on there with my daughter, sometimes for hours, to help with homework, watch her create new dances, learn how to play guitar and piano, write songs, sing, or just to talk. There are so many different stories I could tell that helped me keep my faith and get closer to God. I will admit, the devil has tried to get me in so many ways for most of these twenty years, but I refused to let him win. A few stories that happened in those twenty years had a major impact on me and kept my faith strong.

Being pregnant wasn't easy for me. My firstborn weighed 9½ pounds, which caused muscles and ligaments to be damaged. I had an umbilical hernia while I was pregnant with my second born, which caused tremendous pain, and I ended up having surgery to repair it when my daughter was six weeks old. When I woke up from the anesthesia, I was in terrible pain not only around my abdomen but also in my lower back and legs. I had an MRI four weeks later and was told I had three herniated discs in my lower spine.

Six weeks after the surgery, I was still having horrible pain around my belly button and started noticing I could see stitches coming from the inside of my abdomen. I was shocked by the herniated discs in my back, I'd always had a bulging disc in L5-S1, but I was told that wouldn't cause a herniation. The doctors told me only an injury could have caused the problem, but I didn't have any injuries, or pain for that matter, before the hernia repair.

After three months of dealing with pain in my abdomen after surgery, I was able to convince a new surgeon to go in to see what was going on. When I went in for my six-week checkup, the doctor profusely apologized to me, saying he was so sorry he made me wait so long to go in and make any necessary repairs to the first hernia surgery. He told me I had long stitches poking me everywhere along that first repair, so he redid the repair, and my pain in my abdomen went away. These were the first two surgeries I had, and I thought I was done at that point. Oh boy, was I wrong! I've had seventeen surgeries to date, some minor, some major. Let me tell you about the worst ones I endured and in which God was able to intervene and get me through.

In July of 2003, I started feeling nauseous and sick to my stomach. The pain was achy under my ribs, but it was not excruciating. I went to my family doctor, who ordered a CT scan of my abdomen, to see if there was anything wrong. I was told they didn't find anything wrong. Fast-forward to October of 2003—I was still having the same problem.

I again went for a CT scan of my abdomen, and I again was told there's nothing wrong. Finally, in February of 2004, after getting another CT scan in which I was told nothing was wrong, I asked for a copy of the report they'd received from the radiologist. In the summary the radiologist noted my gallbladder was distended. Nobody ever said anything about that in all the scans I had.

At that point I was miserable. Quite frankly, I was fed up with the constant sickness to my stomach and nausea I'd been dealing with for eight months. I called my friend, who worked for a gastroenterologist. They recommended I make an appointment and come in the following day. The doctor read the report then scheduled me for an endoscopy. If he didn't find anything in my stomach, then he would schedule me for a specialized test for my gallbladder.

The endoscopy went fine, so I had my gallbladder tested the next day. After the test, I asked the technician if they could tell me if they found anything. They told me I should be getting a call from my doctor, probably on the way home, because the gallbladder should be functioning at no less than 32 percent and mine was functioning at 13 percent.

So I get the call from my doctor, who said I needed to see my surgeon that night. I said, "It's four p.m. on Friday afternoon. Good luck with that!" He replied, "No, they'll see you." I got a callback, and my appointment was that night at 6:30 p.m. My surgeon told me my gallbladder needed to come out as soon as possible but asked if I could wait until Monday. I said, "I've been dealing with this for eight months. I guess a few days won't hurt." I was the first person in surgery that day. Once my gallbladder was removed, I felt 100 percent better! No more nausea or feeling sick to my stomach. My surgeon told me my gallbladder was filled with gallstones. How that was missed in the CT is beyond me. All I know is God was with me the eight months I was sick and taking care of a five- and three-year-old the whole time. He then guided me through a successful surgery and healing.

In January of 2015 I started experiencing terrible pains in my stomach, along with other symptoms such as acid indigestion and nausea. After five months of suffering, I finally went into the ER to see if they could figure out the problem. They did a CT scan, diagnosed me with gastritis, and recommended I see a gastroenterologist for an endoscopy of my stomach. When I called their office to set up an appointment, I was told I would need to pay $1,500 toward my deductible in order to have the scan done. I decided to forego the endoscopy, hoping that the Nexium I was given would ease my pain and make it go away.

Unfortunately, that didn't happen. I ended up getting worse, which led me back to the ER now nine months into 2015. Because I had been to the ER four months prior, they wouldn't give me another CT scan to see if there was something else wrong. They again said it was gastritis, sent me home with the same instructions and same medications as before. I can remember sitting there, crying to the doctor, trying to make an argument for him to do another CT scan on me. He refused, saying the meds would work, and he didn't think they would find anything on a CT. So I left and had the prescription filled, praying for relief from my pain. The pain greatly increased throughout the day, and by eight thirty that night, I had my mom call 911. Every step taken and every bump we hit while in the ambulance caused me to scream out from the pain.

The EMT gave me a shot for the pain and said I should start feeling immediate relief. It did not work, and to make matters worse, when I ended up in the ER, they put me in a wheelchair and sat me in the lobby to wait for an open room. I don't know how long I sat there before they called my name, maybe two to three hours. When the ER doctor came in to examine me, he couldn't even touch my abdomen without me screaming. He scheduled me for a CT. During the scan the radiologist wanted me to raise my arms above my head, but I couldn't because the pain was that bad. I got taken back to my room, and not fifteen minutes go by before the doctor is in there with the results of my scan. I had a perforated ulcer in my stomach and needed immediate emergency surgery. It was about 3:00 a.m. when the surgeon got there. He examines me, and they send me right up to the operating rooms.

When I awoke from the surgery, about 10:00 a.m., I was so confused and not sure of my surroundings. A nurse came in and told me I was in the ICU. The first words out of my mouth were "I need to call my employer and let them I won't be in today." I asked for my cell phone and proceeded to call my supervisor to let her know. After my call, I noticed my mom had left a message for me. She wanted to know what had happened in the ER and told me to call her and let her know.

I called, but she wasn't there, and I left a message. Not fifteen minutes later, she showed up in my ICU room with a potted flower plant. She said she had gotten so nervous that she called the hospital, and they had told her I was in the ICU. She freaked out and came right over. When the surgeon came to check on me, he told me I had had a hole in my stomach the size of a half-dollar. He fixed it by cutting out most of my stomach. He also said I had bowel waste pouring into my bloodstream from the hole and I had blood poisoning as a result, which is why I was in the ICU.

It was a very scary time. This is when I first questioned my faith. I had so many surgeries up to that point, and I could not believe God would make me suffer so much. I was a good, kindhearted person, and it didn't make sense. My other thought was why he would cause such a horrible death, if I were to die, seeing how much pain I'd been in over the last fifteen years at that point.

> **It was a very scary time. This is when I first questioned my faith.**

Once I got over my pity party and was moved from the ICU to a regular room, I started to change my tune. I became grateful again to God for helping me live. If I were to die any time soon, I could say it wasn't all bad. I was in the hospital a total of nine days, then I stayed home from work for a week. I then went back to work half days for three weeks.

Although the doctor wanted me out of work for three months, I was a contractor, and I didn't make money unless I worked. While I was in the hospital for those nine days, I had come to the decision that no matter what, I was going to find a way to move back to Maryland. I therefore submitted my résumé to multiple jobs around the DC–Maryland area as a bridge for my move. As I healed from that surgery, my mom became more ill. She all but stopped eating, showering, watching TV, or even playing with the dogs.

Just to give you a little background on my mom: She wasn't always the best mother around. I had dealt with her abusive, neglectful alcohol and drug abuse the first seventeen years of my life. She finally got clean after all those years. Although the addictive behaviors changed, she was still not the easiest person to deal with in my life. I left home in North Carolina when I was eighteen and moved back to Maryland. There I matured over the next eleven years. I felt like I needed to get away. My mom tried to control most of my life, and we didn't get along a lot of the time. However, all that changed soon after I moved back to North Carolina again. We grew closer together during that time. She became the mom I'd always wanted: kind, giving, and staying out of my business unless I asked for her opinion.

During the last year of my mom's life, I was her caretaker. She was sick from congestive heart failure, so I made sure she was fed, and we spent time together. I knew my mom needed me, and at that point, I did not mind. One night a few months before her passing, she ended up in the hospital in the ICU, heavily sedated. She suffered a major heart attack. Her cardiologist tried to put a stent in but was unable because the artery was floppy, and the stent did not stay. He told me this would be a death sentence for my mom, thinking she might not last the week.

She prevailed though. She got better and went to rehab for a week before she threatened to walk home herself just to get out. She also threatened to throw me out of her house, so I went and got her out of the hospital. After about a month, she seemed to be feeling better, but she was back and forth through Christmas. I stayed in her room because she didn't want to interact with my daughter or brother. She kept saying she didn't feel good.

The new year came, and my mom's health seemed to really be improving. I thought, *Whew, I think we dodged a bullet.* Oh boy, was I wrong! On January 24, 2017, I woke up to my same routine of getting ready for work. My mom passed the bathroom and gave me grief over a knob that I couldn't get to stay on the cabinet being on the floor. I called her "old lady" all the time and said, "Oh my gosh, really, at this hour?" I laughed at her, and she walked downstairs.

    I went to work and came home, but I didn't have my key to get into the house because I was using my spare car key. So I called the house to have my mom come open the door—no answer. We had a big picture window that I could look in through when I was walking to the front door. I noticed the TV was on, and I thought maybe she was out back with the dogs or napping in her room. I found the spare key she kept hidden in the leaves by the door and let myself in. While walking to my room, I heard the shower going in her room; I thought, *She must be getting a lot better because she's finally showering like she used to do.*

    So I went into my room to change from work and get her nightly medications. After about fifteen minutes, I came out of my room to give her the meds and still heard the shower running in her bathroom. Two seconds later, it clicked in my brain: something was wrong.

    I ran into her room, threw the meds on her dresser and went to her bathroom. I found her motionless, lying in the shower. She had a stool that she sat on in the shower, and she had fallen backward. The shower water running was cold as ice. I tried pulling her up by her hand to get some type of response or to see if I could help her in any way . . . Nothing.

    I ran to my phone and called 911. I was freaking out on the operator, who was trying to get me to get my mom out of the shower to start CPR. I told the lady that, firstly, I couldn't get her out of the shower because of the way she had fallen, the sliding glass doors was in the way, and it was too tight of a space in the bathroom.

    I told the 911 operator I knew my mom was dead because I had been taken care of her for a while and knew when something was wrong that I could fix. I waited in the hallway until the firemen came. They asked me to go downstairs while they checked her. The police came and went upstairs to observe the situation. Finally, a police officer came down to the living room, where I had been, to tell me that, in fact, my mom had indeed passed. They needed her doctor's number to get them to sign off on the death certificate. I remember crying like I never had before in my entire life. I thought I'd been through the worst in my life and that it wouldn't be such pain. My best friend committed suicide, my oldest brother passed away at forty-three from a massive heart attack, my half-brother passed away at forty-two from small-cell lung cancer, I had lost over twenty friends to cancer, suicide, drugs, and car accidents. How could I have thought there was anything in my life that would cause me such grief now? But there was—my mom.

While dealing with this grief, the executor for my mom's estate decided we needed to sell her home. It was sold before the realtor ever got the sign in the yard. I was told I had three weeks to move out of the house I had lived in for seven years! I was at a crossroads. I wanted to move back to Maryland and be with my kids, but I didn't have a job there yet. I prayed on this very hard, and the decision came easy. I would leave my job in North Carolina to move back to Maryland.

And that's what I did. With every prayer, I took my next steps. They all came easy. A friend of mine found me a room to rent so I could look for work and not have many bills. My roommate was wonderful, and living there was a pleasure. I found a job within three weeks of being back in Maryland, doing what I'd been doing for years so it all came easy. I prayed about leaving that job, and again, the answer came. I found the job I'm currently in, and I'm loving it!

> I found the job I'm currently in, and I'm loving it!

I am so very, very, grateful for everything that has happened in my life. It's been a long journey to get here, but I finally feel like I'm in a good place. And although I've been through all these trying events, my faith became stronger. Now I've found the place I call home.

STORY 23

George O. Topovski

GOD GAVE US life. Jesus gave us salvation and forgave us for the sins we committed. When I was five years old, I watched the soul of a family dog go slowly up into the sky, through the clouds, and up into heaven. The colors were that of a rainbow, and the structure slowly turned into a bubble as it ascended from the ground up into the sky. I was learning about God and Jesus before that and witnessed the dog's passing at my grandparent's house. I felt this was God's way of showing me that the soul of the dog was going to be OK because he was now with God.

A few months later, my grandpa passed away. He had a heart attack while fishing. I was very close to my grandpa. I saw the same light and colors that I did with the dog. Only this time, it was in the funeral home. Believing he was going into heaven, I watched his soul go up through the ceiling. The bubble wasn't as big because it was inside the funeral home.

> **After he passed, I knew God was with me, even at that young age.**

My grandpa Yeagley's passing affected me so severely that I lost strength in my legs and couldn't walk for several weeks. My legs could not hold me. I remember my uncle Gary making me crutches so I didn't have to crawl. I had broken out in hives, and my soul missed my grandpa so much that I became very ill and could not walk. I was only five years old. After he passed, I knew God was with me, even at that young age. However, I got into trouble a lot growing up because I listened to the older kids and I didn't want to pay attention God.

When I was a young teen, my uncle Tom was very sick with a kidney disease causing purpura, where his skin turned purple. He was only ten months older than me, and we were very close. It devastated me to see him so sickly in the hospital for close to a year. We were all praying for my uncle Tom, but he needed a kidney donor fast! Due to previous conditions, he not only needed a donor, he needed someone who was a good match.

It seemingly was too late. He was seventy-seven pounds, and death was at his door. In the late 1960s, it was very time-consuming to test for a donor, and time was of the essence. My grandma contacted the Red Cross who contacted my uncle Mike serving in Germany during the Vietnam War. He came back to the states and was tested to see if he was a good match. However, he had to return to Germany, or he would be AWOL. After he landed in Germany, he was found to be the best match. But now he was in Germany!

Although there were other siblings that might have been a match, both my uncle Tom and uncle Mike had hepatitis, and my uncle Mike was the best match. My twenty-year-old uncle Ken courageously stepped in and contacted the Red Cross. He explained the situation, asking them to intercede and help Uncle Mike return to the states so he could donate his kidney.

At one point, Uncle Tom was in a deep coma for twenty-six days. He was bleeding internally, which caused the purpura, but the doctors were able to stop the bleeding. He went back and forth into a semicoma for almost sixty days. During this period, Uncle Tom would hear the doctors say, "This boy is not going to make it. He is going to die." When my grandma was allowed in the room, my uncle Tom told grandma what the doctors said. She said, "You will not die. You've got to fight!" As Grandma would leave his room, my uncle Tom would repeat, "Fight, fight, fight."

In actuality, most everyone thought he was going to die. He needed the kidney transplant yesterday. They had taken both of his kidneys on July 16, 1969, to prepare him for the transplant. He was on dialysis

> **In actuality, most everyone thought he was going to die.**

and waiting for Uncle Mike to return. I heard there were complications. I was so distraught in my soul that I might lose two uncles that I asked God to take me instead of them. I don't know why it pained me so much. But it did. I just couldn't take it anymore. So I asked God to take me. I wasn't afraid. I just wanted them to be well. But God had another plan.

My uncle Mike made it back to the States just in time to donate his kidney to my uncle Tom. On September 5, 1969, Uncle Tom received the kidney transplant. And although the doctors didn't give much hope, his new kidney worked immediately! He was released from the hospital ten days later.

This was over fifty years ago, and they are both still alive and doing well today. This was miraculous in my eyes. Even though God did not take my life, my uncle Mike gave his kidney to save his brother's life. This was not an easy thing to do in the late sixties. They literally were front-page news! Newspaper articles were written about the entire event, interviewing my grandmother and others. The story was followed by many in the community. This, to me, was a miracle of the family coming together in uncanny circumstances and prayers from everyone who knew us.

Years later, I married and had four children. I had a good job at Ford Motor Company and thought all was well. I thought we were happy. But in an instant, almost like overnight, I lost my wife and kids through a bad divorce. I haven't seen my daughter for over thirty years. Their mom told them I didn't want anything to do with them and I didn't love them. This was a lie that turned into years of pain for everyone. I fought to see my kids through the court system for years. Although the courts said I could see my children, my ex-wife would not allow it. This broke my heart. Yet I still believed in God. I see my oldest two children and their children now. It was faith in God that got me through this torrential downfall, which was right around the same time I also lost my grandmother.

About twenty-six years after my grandpa passed away, my grandma Yeagley was very sick. When I visited her, she pointed to a white light on the wall. She said Jesus and Grandpa were waiting for her, but others wanted her to fight through the sickness. I told her to do whatever she wanted to do. Only she could make that decision, and it was her decision alone. She passed soon after, and I knew she was with Jesus and Grandpa.

One of the last things she said to everyone was, "I want to see all my kids in heaven."

> One of the last things she said to everyone was, "I want to see all of my kids in heaven."

I later remarried and went through a similar situation as my first divorce, but this time it was worse. We had a daughter together who was carefree and sweet. We were visiting my dad one day and as we were leaving, my daughter ran across the street toward the car. But—*BANG!*—she was hit by a car. I ran to her in the middle of the street and instinctively picked her up and rushed her to the hospital, praying to God to save her life. She was Life-Flighted to Cleveland Clinic. She made it through many surgeries that followed, and eventually she came home. I thought we were going to be a happy family. But I was wrong.

To my surprise, during this second marriage, my then wife became involved in witchcraft. This caused many more problems than what we had. I did not like that she was talking to people about séances and other witchcraft activity. It was during this time, while I was mowing the lawn, that my lawnmower rolled over on me and I was taken to the hospital.

I had several broken ribs, hit my head, and had other various injuries. Although I had headaches and migraines in the past, nothing prepared me for what I was about to go through. While in the hospital I had an MRI, CAT scans, and x-rays. This is when they found five cancerous tumors on my brain. This is where the fight for my life really began. Never in a million years could I have known that I was about to have two brain surgeries within a ten-day period.

This is how it happened. The doctor told me I had brain cancer and had less than two weeks to live. He said I could talk with a specialist, and so I did. The specialist told me I had less than a 35 percent chance of surviving

> The doctor told me I had brain cancer and had less than two weeks to live.

the surgery to remove the tumors. I told him that if I only had less than two weeks to live, then it didn't matter if I went now or then. Right before the surgery, I noticed there was a team of ten to twelve doctors in the room. I told the main doctor who was doing my surgery not to worry if I passed away because God was directing his hands. If God wanted me to stay alive, then I would make it through. And if he didn't, then I would be on the other side. I would be in God's hands, no matter what. The doctor did not respond to what I said but had tears in his eyes.

After surgery, several hours later, the surgeon told me that he never had anybody say what I told him before. I told the doctor that I meant it with all my heart and soul. Then he said, once we got in there (into my brain), the cancer was gone. Instead of cancer, it was an infection. Even though the MRI, blood work, and other tests showed it was cancer. The doctor said it was unexplainable. They removed the infection at the base of my skull where two of the tumors lay on my brain. They did not feel they needed to remove the other three tumors, but rather they would drain them at a later time if needed.

I was sent home eight days after the surgery. The ninth day after surgery, I had excruciating pain in my head due to cigarette smoke in the house. I went back to Akron General Hospital, and the doctors took out the other three tumors in the front of my brain. This is when I died six times, and they brought me back to life.

> **During this time, while I was in heaven with the Lord, I asked him if I could see heaven and hell.**

During this time, while I was in heaven with the Lord, I asked him if I could see heaven and hell. He first showed me a glimpse of heaven. It was very beautiful. He brought to me my grandma and grandpa Yeagley. They told me everything was going to be all right.

Then he showed me a glimpse of hell. I saw a fiery pit with smoke. It was hot—very hot—and loud and noisy. There were lots of screams and hollering. I couldn't make any sense out of what was being screamed. I felt all hate was there. Nobody liked it, and I felt the souls wanted out of the chaos. I knew the souls in the fire wanted out. They did not want to be there, and there wasn't anything they could do about it. I felt as if they might have been asking me to take them with me out of hell. But I couldn't. Then I came back to life and was in the recovery room. I didn't realize it at the time, but I was paralyzed from the neck down.

The doctors never expected me to walk again. The circulation in my legs was not working properly. If I had my legs propped up, I was OK. But when they were bent at my knees, the pain was unbearable. It took me over a year to learn how to walk again.

The activity with my wife became worse. When I began to walk, I filed for and got a divorce. This was when I did not see my then eleven-year-old daughter for over six years because my ex told the court she was afraid of me. There were no reasons given, but the court denied me rights to my daughter. I was only able to write to my daughter. I believe she did not get all my letters because I asked her when I started to see her again. That was when she told me she only received a couple of my letters.

After my second divorce, I started making better decisions. It has been over fifteen years since my brain surgery, and I am still walking. I give God all the glory for what he has seen me through. My faith is stronger. I now write "God loves you" on every bill I hand out. It is my secret ministry, a way I can help tell or remind people that God loves them. I give all the glory to God, and I want people to know that God is good. He is always with them, and he loves them very much.

STORY 24

Joel Sibbalds

I THOUGHT I DIED. Adrenaline rushed through my body, and a bright white light was all my eyes could take in. I also couldn't hear anything except the sound of ringing. The only thing I could think was, *I have to get back up.* I could feel the rough concrete beneath me as I began moving. Moving was good. That meant I was alive. I was getting back up to walk over to the ladder when, suddenly, arms wrapped around me as a voice told me, "Oh no you don't." It was Jerry, Lydia's dad.

> **I thought I died. Adrenaline rushed through my body, and a bright white light was all my eyes could take in.**

I still wanted to get up and get back to work, but my body, feeling as weak as it was, allowed him to bring me back down and rest against him. *I shouldn't be here. This shouldn't have happened to me. Why did I volunteer to help fix up her parent's roof?* I was tired, sweaty, and my arms were scratched up from the shingles. I originally thought that was uncomfortable, but then, as I tried to move, my face, wrists, and leg hurt simultaneously.

I had been helping Lydia's brother with the roofing felt. I was just trying to do my part and be a good boyfriend. We had been at one of the highest points on the house. I remember being told to roll out the felt, and her brother would staple it down. All I was focused on was roll, pause, staple, roll, pause, staple. The house had a few more feet to go, or so I thought. I had stepped off the roof, the felt ripping and coming down with me. I don't know how I managed to turn belly side down during the fall, but I'm thankful I managed, or I wouldn't be walking today.

I had hit the ground in less than five seconds, but it felt like years. I was falling in slow motion, and I can remember looking out over their fence into the field behind their house. We had been working all weekend in the hot sun about two stories up, but now I was lying on the ground, adrenaline slowly leaving me. I felt so tired and was starting to doze off, but soon after, my vision started coming back to me. I looked down and all around me. Everything was blurry, and blood was dripping from my face.

The sounds of screaming started to replace the ringing sound. It felt like I was drowning in all the noise; the screaming so loud it was piercing my ears. Then, all I heard for what seemed like hours was the ambulance sirens. The EMTs arrived and had brought a stretcher over to me. They were asking me a lot of questions, but I don't remember answering them from feeling so exhausted.

Once the neck brace was on, my ribs had been checked, and they knew I could feel and move my legs, they were ready to place me on the stretcher. On the count of three, they were going to lift me, so I had to brace for pain. When they said "Three," I felt everything that had happened to me. In the middle of them pushing and pulling, I blurted, "Please fix me!" The pain in my wrists were unbearable, and for some reason, it was hard to open my jaw to scream.

They had put medication in me to help relieve my pain, and I finally felt like I could rest. I remember dreaming of a man telling me, "This isn't the end." I went through all kinds of x-rays and scans for over eight hours. I remember being told, "Breathe in, breathe out," "Hold your breath, and stay still." While that was going on, it felt as though something was attracting me to look to the corner of the room. Once I focused on the corner, I saw my grandmother, who had passed away when I was a toddler. She had a warm smile on her face. Tears started to fall from my eyes, which caused me to close them. She wasn't there when I reopened them.

> I could remember all the things I knew he helped me with during my life up to this point.

I believed in God, but I never talked or prayed to him for anything. I never felt that I needed help from him. In that moment, however, I thanked God for being there for me, for keeping me with Lydia, and so I could see my family again. I also thanked him for the chance to see my grandma again. It was a blessing, and I could remember all the things I knew he helped me with during my life up to this point. I went through a lot more in the hospital, but this is what pulled me closest to God. It made me realize that I could withstand anything if I had faith in God and remember that he didn't put me in this situation, but he helped bring me through it.

STORY 25

Juanita Teasley

I DID NOT GROW up in church, but I did grow up in a family that proclaimed their love for GOD. They grew up in the church but were in their retirement years when I was a child. I remember the Lord's Prayer up on every entrance way in our home. All the same, I have often felt that if I had grown up knowing the LORD, I would have had an easier life and made better decisions.

> I did not grow up in church, but I did grow up in a family that proclaimed their love for GOD.

The first time I had heard anything about Jesus or GOD was around seven years old. I was standing by the coat closet directly in front of the front door. My cousin Glenda had asked my grandmother if she could take me to church with her. I was daydreaming at the time. However, that caught my attention when they began discussing GOD. I remember asking, "Who is GOD?" My grandmother replied, "He made you." Ever since then, I had a desire to know more about HIM.

However, the next opportunity to meet GOD that I can remember was in high school. My friend Rebecca had invited me to church with her family. I was about sixteen. It was a Catholic church, and the experience was such a quick one. It did not leave any other impression on me. At this point, I still did not know GOD.

Later, around the age of nineteen, a guy I had been dating from high school invited me to his church, New Salem Baptist Church. This was approximately in 1992. It was at this church that it was first explained to me who Jesus is, his character, etc. I remembered hearing GOD, but I really didn't know anything about Jesus. I remember going to church late every time I went, and drastically late to boot. One time or two, I witnessed the movement of GOD, but I didn't know what was going on. This was a big church, and the members in the sanctuary were hollering out, praising GOD, and thanking HIM. They were excited. I wondered why I did not feel just a little bit of what they were experiencing. It puzzled me.

Furthermore, I continued to feel separated from the experience even after I was baptized. It got to a point where I knew everything the pastor was going to say next. I had thought about quitting church, but my spirit encouraged me to become involved in ministry so I could help make a difference by encouraging something new. I did not respond right away. Consequently, life got the best of me, and I backslid for about a decade.

The odd thing is, I did not know I was backsliding until after I had rejoined the church. During this time, there were several life events that permanently changed my life. My natural mother died, and my grandmother (adoptive mother) died one year after. Other things happened too.

I fell into a depression but didn't know it. Back then I did not believe in depression. The folks I heard using the word seemed to be exaggerating and used the term loosely. I did not have firsthand experience with it, and no book could have helped me understand it better than real life. I remember living in the dark. I remember not eating at all. I remember avoiding my family, friends, and coworker friends. I don't know how I didn't lose everything.

I don't remember paying my bills. I didn't go grocery shopping; I didn't check the mail. What I do remember is barely making it to work every day. I remember parking at the same meter. My car had gotten towed a least three times a week. Folks I didn't even know who would ask me, "You have the Mazda? Your car was towed again."

> **I did not have the energy to care.**

I did not have the energy to care. I was just going through the motions. However, even in a depressed state, I was never suicidal. I could not see beyond my circumstances. I imagined I would feel that way forever. But GOD had a different plan for my life!

One day I ran into a children's Bible I had picked up. I had planned to read it. After about a month, I had completed reading the entire book. It made an impression on me. This encouraged me to be hopeful. I hoped for a better day. I hoped to fill the void in me with something meaningful. I had hoped to overcome my circumstances and the dysfunction of my family. I hoped for a good life with good and positive people around me. It took a while, but eventually I mustered up the follow-through to return to church.

But it was the same thing. I knew exactly what the pastor was going to say next. Finally, I asked a member, "How do I get involved with the choir?" I was told to just show up to a rehearsal on a Wednesday and introduce myself. So I did. Before I knew it, GOD delivered me from depression. He also delivered me from a heart that hates. I practice forgiveness daily.

Since then GOD has blessed me with joy. Now things that used to bother me, I don't respond to them in the same way anymore. I have learned how to talk (pray) to GOD. I now experience GOD through praise and worship. I know Emmanuel is with me all day, every day! GOD has helped me to understand his multiple characteristics. It blows my mind, because on a regular basis, I literally learn something new about Jesus every day.

I did not know Jesus is the door to heaven; I always called him the bridge back to GOD. I did not know that he made us; I thought the FATHER made us. Now I know GOD as a healer. I have a personal relationship with GOD. I now know that GOD chose me before I chose HIM. Needless to say, living to be more pleasing to GOD, is a lifestyle. I believe GOD is preparing me now for my place in the afterlife. Looking back to the beginning in Genesis there was always praise, worship, and singing with the church.

> **I now know that GOD chose me before I chose HIM.**

To GOD be the glory.

STORY 26

LaKesha Cunningham

Walking Testimony

THERE ARE MANY things that I could testify about, and this is one of my stories. I had been dealing with acid reflux like millions of Americans. I had, and was taking, the maintenance medicines. However, my condition started to get progressively worse. I began swallow studies and endoscopies to find the problem issue. It had gotten to the point where food and acid would come out of my nose. I was told I had a paraesophageal hernia, which sat behind my esophagus. It started to twist one day, and I ended up in the hospital and surgery was scheduled.

I believed I had a top-notch doctor. He was a thoracic cardiac surgeon. The best of the best in my mind. Well, fast-forward to the surgery. Instead of doing the surgery laparoscopically, he did a procedure called a thoracotomy. This is the same type of surgery used for lung transplants. So he went in through my back, cracked two ribs, and cut through some nerves and muscles. I ended up with two chest tubes, three IVs, a gastric tube stitched to my nose, and on and on. I was in the cardiac ICU for eight days, and according to my father, I looked like I was going to go at any minute.

> **I told him, "OK, Lord, we can do this. It isn't our first one, and you have brought me through others. You will bring me through this one too."**

While admitted, the pain was like nothing imagined. I was told it is the most painful surgery someone could go through. During the night, when I couldn't handle the pain, I would just start talking to God. I told him, "OK, Lord, we can do this. It isn't our first one, and you have brought me through others. You will bring me through this one too."

The Lord sent me two angels, which were my beautiful children and support system. The day I was discharged from the hospital, my then husband did not take me home. My son walked from the hospital to our house, and with just a temporary driver's permit, he got my car and picked me up. My children nursed me through the most painful and traumatic surgery I would ever face. They never complained or missed a beat. They made sure my wounds were changed and dressed, they made me meals—they gave me anything I needed. Needless to say, I am no longer married, but that is a blessed story for another day. My children, now sixteen and twenty-one years old, are still my support system and nurses. I have been truly blessed with them. I praise God for choosing me to be their mother.

After being discharged I noticed I began vomiting up food from three days prior. I called the surgeon and was told I may have a blockage. I went back to testing to look for the issue. I finally ended up going to the Cleveland Clinic and was told I had gastroparesis. This is a condition where the stomach is partially paralyzed, and it cannot contract to digest food. This condition was caused by that doctor cutting the vagus nerve on my stomach, which controls not only my stomach but my nervous system, my brain, as well as my heart.

This meant the food that went down just sat in my stomach. It would rot until I became sick and would just start throwing up. I couldn't control when I would throw up or have diarrhea. This continued for almost two years until another corrective surgery was scheduled.

When I came through an almost total gastrectomy with Roux-en-Y to remove almost all of my paralyzed stomach, I was told by the surgeon that the original surgeon who performed my thoracotomy had stitched my stomach up into my chest and he had to get it loose in order to correct it.

Now you tell me how you can live with your stomach stitched in your chest for nearly two years. No feeding tubes, no hospitalizations.

The mercy and grace of God kept me moving and living until my new surgeon could go in and fix what my previous surgeon had done.

People with gastroparesis usually end up on feeding tubes and in the hospital due to the inability to thrive. I still have some complications from that one single surgery even to this day. Because that nerve was cut, I now suffer from malabsorption. Which means, my body cannot absorb the vitamins from food. I had to undergo IV iron infusions because I had almost no iron in my body and vitamin supplements wouldn't give me enough iron. That issue coupled with losing so much blood during my menstrual cycle led me to have a total hysterectomy in January of 2019.

> **Regardless of all that has happened to me, I give God all the glory for keeping me alive.**

Regardless of all that has happened to me, I give God all the glory for keeping me alive. Although I have been through so many things and can still sit here to talk about it means I have a purpose. One thing I am confident of: my health will not take me until he says so.

STORY 27

Jamal McClendon

WE ALL HAVE very tough times. We have ways in which we think everything is over and have no possibility of seeing the light at the end of the tunnel. I recall there was one time when I knew I would never be able to see the light at the end of the tunnel. And I am here to tell you that story.

Back around February of 2018, I lost someone whom I thought I was supposed to spend the rest of my life with. In obliquity to what I thought was going to happen, God had other plans. God shows signs, and it is up to us to see these signs. Me personally, I ignored all signs that this person was not right for me. I tried to take the next journey into my life by becoming one in holy matrimony at least three times, but every time, something got in my way. These signs were God telling me, "This isn't the person for you, Jamal." But ignored them and paid the price.

Once we parted ways, I was a wreck. Everyone mourns for a short time, but I thought I could not stop mourning. I lost what I thought was everything, I lost my job, and I lost my best friend—all in the course of two months. When I reached this lowest point. I no longer had a clear path of where my life was going. I knew it was over. I knew that there was only one way out of this. I doubted my belief in God. I doubted everything that he had done for me.

When I reached this lowest point, something came over me that I had never felt before. It was in the presence of some sort, and all I could feel or think was, *It's not over.* I kept hearing, "It's not over. If you've got air to breathe it's not over." It said, "You're a

> I kept hearing, "It's not over. If you've got air to breathe, it's not over."

fighter. You have something better coming. So get up, because it is not over." After this, I took a different look at things. I looked closer and saw that this didn't kill me. I could have let it consume me, but I didn't. It made me stronger.

Once this presence gave me a better outlook on life, God opened many doors for me. He helped me find a way out of this dark place I was in. He began to show me my path again. It might not have been my original choice, but it was a path he had planned for me. I have learned from this experience that sometimes I must let God take control. I can't do everything on my own.

We all have a path in life. We meet people along the way. We learn a few lessons from them along the way. We have seasonal friends and lifetime friends. God puts those people in our life for reason. We all must grasp and see which people in our lives are seasonal friends or lifetime friends. When we mix these people up, we begin to stray from our path because we want to bring these people with us. God has a plan for these people like he has a plan for us.

We must let go. We are allowed to worry about it, we can even stress about it, but over and over, the words "Trust God" will always get us through it.

STORY 28

Candace Williams

"AND WE KNOW that ALL things work together for good to those who love God, to those who are called according to his purpose" (Romans 8:28 NKJV, emphasis mine).

Monster, horrible mother, junkie, obese, insecure, codependent, victim of manipulation, sexual abuse, mental, and physically abused victim. This is how many across the nation in June of 2009 viewed me. If I am honest, I identified myself as all these adjectives and even more explicit things.

My name is Candace Williams (Watson). On June 24, 2009, the Lord met me in the most peculiar place: a 4 × 9 isolated jail cell. I encountered peace beyond my understanding in that 4 × 9 cell. It was only me and a Bible, because that was all they permitted me to have. "Don't be surprised at the fiery trials you are going through, as if something strange were happening to you," 1 Peter 4:12 NKJV. It was in that 4 × 9 cell that the Lord showed me why I had endured and survived all that I had in my life through one Bible verse, Romans 8:28.

> On June 24, 2009, the Lord met me in the most peculiar place: a 4 × 9 isolated jail cell.

The Lord knew me in my mother's womb and that I was worth saving because one day I would be used to widen his kingdom. I believe that my whole life, satan has been trying to take me out. As stated above, the Lord knew I was worth saving despite the attacks of the enemy. While I was in my mother's womb, there was extensive abuse she endured as well as suicidal attempts. This was where my journey of abandonment, abuse, lack of self-worth, and the many other lies of the enemy all began, in my mother's womb. "Before I formed you in the womb, I knew you; Before you were born, I sanctified you; I ordained you a prophet to the nations" (Jeremiah 1:5 NKJV).

On July 19, 1984, I made a grand entrance to a mother who suffered from addiction and a father I would later discover is more than likely not my biological father, due to him being incarcerated at the time of my conception. A bastard child, as the world would claim. "I will be a father to you, and you shall be my sons and daughters, says the Lord Almighty" (2 Corinthians 6:18 NKJV).

My childhood is mostly a blur. I remember bits and pieces, both good and bad. I know this is probably for my protection. All attacks from the enemy were to implement an identity I would carry around for many years. I moved many times in my childhood. I know this effected my ability to bond and build relationships. I had abandonment issues as well as a survival mindset.

I had no clue how to deal with emotions. I would go from being emotionless to a raging ball of emotions. I was later diagnosed with bipolar, manic depression, PTSD, and anxiety. Through these younger years, there were many nights my brothers and I endured being ignored so the adults around us could party. We always seemed to be thrown under the rug, and my mom chose men and drugs over us, her kids. From my understanding, this was the same behavior my grandmother also displayed for my mother. I knew firsthand that an apple does not fall far from the tree it was produced from. I knew in my heart this was a generational curse, a cycle, that had to be broken and not passed along.

> **Being pregnant set off a light bulb that the way I was being treated was not right.**

I was abused sexually my entire childhood. At the age of fifteen, I left home thinking I could get away from the abuse. Unfortunately, the sexual abuse pattern continued. I was cheated on. I was pulled down the stairs by my hair and punched in the face. I did not know any better. I wanted out but didn't know how to get out. Instead of me being treated the way God wants a woman to be treated, the learned behavior (generational curse/cycle) continued. This learned behavior continued in me because

I didn't know my worth and accepted whatever attention I could get. This went on for years. By God's grace I graduated high school and began college. Soon after, I became pregnant. Being pregnant set off a light bulb that the way I was being treated was not right.

I had some friends in Arizona who said I could come live with them. Four short weeks after having my beautiful daughter, I packed my little Dodge Neon up with what I thought was important and drove straight through to Phoenix, Arizona. I was twenty years old and had a four-week-old baby girl. In a whole new setting, I felt I had the world at my fingertips. I got a job, started school, and had my own place within a couple months of being there. I loved Arizona until the partying scene was introduced into my life.

Being promiscuous ran rampant in my life. Addiction grabbed a hold of me before I even knew what happened. It began with one sip of alcohol, which later turned into an every-weekend event. As soon as I got off work, I would start drinking. A young man in my apartment complex introduced me to methamphetamines at this time. I did one line and was hooked. My voids were being filled, so I thought.

For years I fought this grip with all my might. In my mind I wanted to do everything in my power not to turn and follow in my mother's footsteps. I had experienced firsthand what drugs do to our family. Drugs and satan had a grip on me that wouldn't loosen. For close to five long years I fought the battle of this grip. Through those years I endured things that most would die from or never come back from.

> **For years I fought this grip with all my might.**

I would stay awake for days on end. At one point I stayed awake for seventeen days. I used drugs with doctors and nurses. I was involved with gang members and drug dealers. I had guns pulled to my head. I attempted suicide three times and was hospitalized several times. I drove and worked while under the influence. I was raped due to situations I put myself in or was too inebriated to even say no. I had three car accidents—one involving a semitruck, which resulted in emergency back surgery. This almost paralyzed me. I had friends die from gunshot wounds, overdoses, and suicides. The picture is painted of how the grip of drugs and satan was so tight on me. I thought and felt as if I would never get away. I felt like satan was choking me and any breath I had left in me. I moved back and forth from Arizona to Ohio several times, attempting to have the grip loosen, even if it was just a little. These grips never loosened. They only got tighter.

This brings me to May of 2009, while in Ohio. My daughter was four years old at this time. I was clean from meth, but still used Adderall and was drinking alcohol. The addiction's grip was still there, and it continued to call my name. I wanted to go back to Arizona so bad, and my body craved it. My daughter's dad and I had tried to work things out and planned on getting married. Then I found out he was cheating on me. This threw me over the edge, not that I was hanging on by a thick rope anyway. He called me one night to pick up a friend of his and asked me to take him a couple places. I did, no questions asked, because it involved receiving money. I could get my fix and feed the demon in me. The guy and I hit it off immediately. After hanging out for a couple days, he had asked me to drive him out west. Oh, how I had been waiting for an excuse to go back out west, and here was my opportunity.

It became like a big escapade or adventure for my daughter and me. So off to the west we went. A bag of clothes and what money we both had together, in a 1998 Chevy Silverado Z74 truck. The deal was he would drop us off in Arizona. But he didn't. I was asleep when he drove through Arizona, and we ended up in California. I do recall stopping at a rest area, looking at the Most Wanted pictures, joking around, saying that would be funny if that was us.

He didn't let us watch TV or listen to the radio. Which I now know why, we were national news on every news station across the country as well as *Nancy Grace* and *America's Most Wanted*. Guess why? Because the guy my daughter and I were with was an escaped tier-3 sex offender.

A couple weeks went by, and so did the money. All I could think about was when I could get high, not what was going on around me. He found a ranch we could stay on if we worked. The women did house chores and took care of the children, while the men worked picking avocados. When we arrived we discovered it was a Christian ranch. I honestly can't tell you how long we stayed there—a week, maybe two. I began to feel uneasy and felt something was wrong with the guy because he became very controlling over who I talked to. I didn't feel comfortable leaving my daughter with him alone. Although I thought I was just going through the motions of praying and worshipping, something was happening within me. "Not by might, nor by power, but by my spirit, says the Lord" (Zechariah 4:6 NIV).

> "Father God, I don't even know who you are or if you even exist, but I cannot live like this anymore."

The Lord was stirring up things within me and loosening that grip which I felt Satan had on me for so long. The cravings I had to use drugs and be back in Arizona just went away. The most vivid thing that I remember is getting on my knees the night of June 23, 2009, and praying these exact words, "Father God, I don't even know who you are or if you even exist, but I cannot live like this anymore." The next morning, I woke up and knew I didn't have to live in the grips of satan any longer. We were surrounded by US marshals and federal agents, guns were pulled, and we were arrested. I found out later that the guy I was with on this month-long escapade had escaped from a halfway house.

I praise God daily that my daughter and I were protected. I was later sentenced to prison time, and my daughter was adopted due to the case being high profile and the extent of the possible danger I allowed my daughter to encounter. Through this time, the Lord had me sitting still in a prison cell. He began to reveal visions for ministries to me. My relationship with him grew, and the identity I had before the day I was arrested had been completely diminished and replaced with a brand-new identity. Satan no longer had a grip on me. I became the daughter of the Most High King, adopted into a royal priesthood. "Therefore, if anyone is in Christ, he is a new creation; old things have passed away; behold, all things have become new" (1 Corinthians 5:17 NKJV).

On July 2011, I was released from prison. I immediately found a church to attend as well as meetings. I thought finding employment would be hard, but the Lord had favor on me and showed me what he meant by moving mountains. I had always worked in the medical field and was prompted by a caseworker to at least try to apply at nursing homes. So I did. I not only gained employment at one but two facilities, working full-time positions. The one facility, I had worked prior to being arrested and during my interview the director of nursing told me that she believed in second chances. It was almost like the felony placed on my record didn't exist. I worked diligently and faithfully at this nursing home, and I still do as a PRN position.

I grew tremendously and learned many skills there. Given the opportunity to move up into management as activity director, and the facility paid for me to get my certification and license as a recreational therapist. All these skills are being used today in ministry. Today, I am married to my wonderful husband, Charles. Our marriage is a testimony on how if the Lord is the center, you have no choice but to grow closer together. I no longer allow myself to be labeled with bipolar, manic depression, PTSD, or anxiety. I have been completely delivered of these labels and take no medications for them.

> **All these skills are being used today in ministry.**

My Brother

Recently, my younger brother Cameron passed away in a car accident. Only one year, almost to the day, he had been shot in the head, missing his brain and spinal cord by a millimeter. The Lord had a hedge of protection around him. I remember getting the phone call that he had been shot and Life-Flighted. Again, an overwhelming peace that I cannot explain came over me. I was able to drive over an hour away to pick up my mother and drive another hour to the hospital. I was able to watch him begin to seek the Lord and witness him being baptized.

My brother had a heart of gold and would give anyone the shirt off his back. He would give you the last bit of food to eat and allow himself to go hungry. The night of his car accident, there was a similar scenario. I received a phone call that he had been Life-Flighted to a trauma unit.

That same overwhelming peace that is indescribable came over me. The difference this time was, I had a vision of the car accident and him being lifted off the pavement and turning into a dove. The Holy Spirit had comforted me and let me know he was with our Father. I later found out that he had in fact died at the scene of the accident but was revived by MedFlight. "And the peace of God, which transcends all understanding, will guard your hearts and your minds in Christ Jesus" (Philippians 4:7 NKJV).

Ministry

> **He had promised that my life would be used as a testimony to bring other women out of the darkness that I once was in.**

Remember, I said the Lord had begun instilling me with visions for ministries? He had promised that my life would be used as a testimony to bring other women out of the darkness that I once was in, that my life would be used to glorify him. Through those promises, Rubies—which comes from Proverbs 31:10 NIV, "She is worth far more than rubies"—was formed.

Rubies is a faith-based women's facility, which houses women who are coming out of the bondage of addiction and/or sex trafficking. Once a woman finds her worth in Christ, like me, everything in her life changes. The Porch Ministry is also flourishing currently. The Porch is a respite center where women who are in bondage to prostitution and human sex trafficking can come and find rest. A woman can be loved in the way Jesus loves. She can be fed physically and spiritually. The vision is that the women will begin to trust enough that they will ask for help and be delivered.

The Porch was put in place after my husband and I both continued to hear about porches. We were curious and wanted to know what exactly a porch was in the Bible. The Lord took us right to the book of Acts. "And through the hands of the apostles many signs and wonders were done among the people. And they were all with one accord in Solomon's Porch," Acts 5:12, NKJV.

When we went searching in our Bibles, I was amazed at what I found. You see, my Bible is a Women's Study Bible, which I had given to my mother-in-law before she had passed away on September 9, 2016. The only verses in this Bible she had highlighted were Acts 3:11–18. These verses are about the healing and preaching that the disciples did on Solomon's Porch. We knew without a doubt that the Lord was calling us to begin the Porch so signs and wonders of deliverance and healing of these women could occur.

May the Glory of my life trials, tribulations, prospering, vision, and ministries all go to the Lord. If you do not know Jesus Christ as your Lord and Savior but would like to, please read Romans 10:9 and ask the Lord into your heart and confess your sins. Being a faithful servant of Jesus Christ is not always easy or trial-free, but I can tell you that you will have more joy, peace, purpose, and praise in your life than can be explained.

> **If you would like more information or feel led to donate to Rubies and/or the Porch, or both please e-mail rubiesoutreach31@gmail.com.**

STORY 29

Rhonda Stewart

My Soul Is Light, My Heart Is Free

LOSING A CHILD is never easy. I have lost two. It has been almost thirty-five years for one son and twenty-five years for another son. I can say the pain of loss is still present, but my soul is light. You see, I believe in God, and I believe there are purposes and lessons to learn for everything that happens in my life. What could the purpose or lessons be you ask? Let me tell you my story.

Thirty-five years ago, I went into labor at a gestation period of six months. I was taken by ambulance which was one hour and forty-five minutes away from my home. It was the closest hospital specializing in neonatal care, and they had a neonatal intensive care unit (NICU). This is what I needed if my child was to have any chance of survival. I started praying. Praying is comforting. It helped to ease my mind and my troubled heart.

The doctors tried to stop the early onset of labor with medication. Unfortunately, it did not work. I prayed, "God, help my baby." I prayed my baby would live and would not have any handicaps. "But if it is your will, God, that my child does not live, help me to accept your will." My child, a son, was born. My prayers were answered. He was one pound, seven ounces at birth. When he was born, I heard him cry.

It would be months before I heard him make another sound. His lungs were underdeveloped, as were other organs. The

> **It seemed like he had tubes everywhere, but by the grace of God, he was here.**

greatest concern was for his lungs. He was in an incubator, and a machine was breathing for him. It seemed like he had tubes everywhere, but by the grace of God, he was here. I loved him from the moment I heard him cry—OK, when I found out I was pregnant, of course, as any mother would.

He was doing well in the NICU. He had worked his way down from 100 percent oxygen with the machine breathing for him to 50 percent oxygen and 50 percent air. Yes, there were ups and downs, but mainly he was improving. His weight had increased to five pounds, and there was talk about him coming home. I was so excited. I thanked the Lord because I knew he was the reason my son had been getting healthier and stronger. We just needed him to be able to breathe 100 percent on his own. The prognosis was good. No, it was great! Everything was working out. Prayers work. I visited him every chance I could.

One of the most memorable visits was in late August. I was talking to him, and he was alert. He would lift the corners of his mouth a bit, and it looked like he was smiling. Of course, he still had the tube in his mouth, but it looked like a smile to me. Then a nurse came by, and it seemed that as soon as he heard her voice, he shut his eyes and pretended to be sleep. When she left, he opened his eyes back up and smiled. His primary nurse was there too. She said he did not like the other nurse because she was always doing something painful like drawing blood or changing his tubes. I thought that was hilarious. He could not talk but he could register his displeasure by that simple act.

One day I received a call from the hospital. It was my son's doctor. My son had taken a turn for the worse. He had double pneumonia, and the machine was again breathing 100 percent for him. His organs were starting to shut down. I was panicked. I was one hour and forty-five minutes away. I got in my car, and I began to pray. I prayed that my son would overcome this too. He overcame a lot. We were talking about taking him home in a few weeks. "Lord, what happened?"

My mind was racing, and so was my car. I prayed, "Lord, help me get to my son safely. Let me be there if or when he dies. I do not want him to die alone. If you must take him home today, give me strength and courage to accept what cannot be changed. You know what is in my heart. I bow to you."

I made it to the hospital in one piece. God was taking care of me. I was calm yet apprehensive. I went to see my son. He was in bad shape. His skin was darkening because of the lack of oxygen. His stomach was extended. His organs were shutting down. I still had hope, and I was praying, always praying. Then his doctor came to see me. By that time my parents had arrived as well. I come from a praying family. They called some friends, and there was a prayer circle for my son, me, and my family.

The doctor wanted to discuss next steps. The prognosis was not good. He discussed my options. I could let him stay on the ventilator while his organs continued to shut down one by one. There was no telling how long that would take. The doctor said he had seen a case where the baby lingered for three days. Or I could take him off the ventilator. They would give him some medicine so he would not be in pain. It was inevitable that my son was going to die. If not today, then maybe tomorrow or the next day.

> **I prayed for the strength to make the right decision, a decision that I would live with for the rest of my life.**

I prayed for the strength to make the right decision, a decision that I would live with for the rest of my life. "Lord, take this heartache away. Let me find peace in my decision. Guide me to what is right for my son and for me." Then I heard a voice.

"We cry, and we are sad for what we are going to miss when someone dies. Do not be selfish and let him linger on. If he is meant to live, he will breathe on his own." I closed my eyes and took a breath. I decided to take him off the respirator. I believe that I showed my son how much I loved him by letting him go. I did what was best for him, not what was best for me and for the grief which was threating to overtake me. I asked God to help me brave the grief of my decision.

The prayer circle was at work. I began to feel lighter. My heart did not feel as heavy. I knew I made the right decision. Looking back to all those years ago, I still know I made the right decision. I put my faith and trust in God.

I asked the doctor if we could take my son outside; there was a little garden. He lived for six months in the NICU. He had never known anything but the NICU. I wanted the sun to kiss his face. The doctor agreed. It was a warm October afternoon. His nurse wheeled his incubator out into that sunny garden. It was quiet and peaceful. We could hear the birds singing. I could feel God's presence even more. I knew he had wrapped me in his loving embrace. I was not alone, nor was I lonely.

I was calm and collective while they unhooked my son from the life-giving machine. I heard him cry. I only heard him cry twice. Once when he was born, and once just before he died. It is strange when I think of that now, but it is one of the memories that I treasure. His nurse placed him in my arms, and there was silence. Nothing existed but me, my son, and God. I was still praying that he would breathe on his own and would live, but I also knew that was not what was meant to be.

As I prayed for this miracle, my prayers began to change. I was praying that God would take my son back into his loving arms until the day I could reunite with him. I prayed that he would give me peace. Peace in my decision, peace in my thoughts and most importantly, peace in my soul. The tightening in my chest started to dissipate. My soul started feeling lighter. I told my son it was OK to let go. Mommy loved him. Mommy would always love him, and one day I would see him again. He looked at me, and he slowly closed his eyes for the last time.

You see, I believe in God. And I believe there are purposes and lessons to be learned for everything that happens in my life. So the original question was, "What could the purpose or lessons be?" My story does not have an ending. You see the purpose is the story that I can tell other people who struggle with the loss of a child. It has been almost thirty-five years. I think of him often. My soul is light, my heart is free, and by the grace of God, I am doing well. One day, you will too. Here is a poem I find comforting:

God's Lent Child
(Unknown Author)

"I'll lend you for a little while
A child of mine," God said—
"For you to love while he lives.
And mourn for when he's dead . . .
But should the angels call for him
Much sooner than we planned,
We'll brave the grief that comes
And try to understand."

LU ANN TOPOVSKI

STORY 30

Sabrina Stump

GOD HAS HAD his hand on my life for as long as I can remember. Ever since I was young, he has been present. Sometimes it was a small subtle thing throughout my day. Sometimes it was over a long period, during certain situations. I knew I would not have made it through had he not been with me. Sometimes, on those special occasions, it was a huge in-my-face, beyond-all-doubt, "I am here, ever present, always in control, you are mine, and I have got you!" kind of moment. Those are the moments that changed me forever. These moments helped me never forget who he is. That shaped me from that day forward. These are two of those moments I have been blessed to have experienced.

> "I am here, ever present, always in control, you are mine, and I have got you!"

Since I was young, my mom had me in church as often as she could. Even when we couldn't go on a regular basis, we still read the Bible, had discussions, prayed every night, and had a relationship with the Lord. He was a regular part of my life, and I believed in him. Now, my mom used to say that there is a difference in *believing* in something and *knowing* it. I think that is true. Because when I simply believe something to be true, there is a possibility that I could be proven wrong. But when I know . . . well, then nothing anyone can say or do can make me know otherwise. It is simply a fact. Looking back now, at all I have been through in my life, I think God wanted me to know from a very young age that he was real and in control. I knew nothing I would go through in my life could ever change that. It's a good thing, because—whew! But we have all been through some stuff. Right?

When I was seven years old, my mom helped my uncle part-time with his business. He had come up with a solution to wipe on leather that protected it and made it waterproof. He had patented it, bottled it, and sold it in various markets. In this specific incident, he and my mom were taking it to a boat show in Florida to sell. They were going to be gone for a week, so my uncle's wife, my aunt, was going to watch me and my brother. So I packed my things, enough for a week, and off to my aunt and uncle's I went. I said goodbye to my mom and uncle as they drove off and was settled in for the week.

At the beginning of our week with her, my aunt took me, my brother, and her son over to her sister's house for the day to visit and play with her children. They had a big fenced-in backyard that was surrounded by a wooded area. There was lots of room to run and play. We were outside much of the day. One day we had a game of kickball going. It was my turn to kick, and I kicked the ball sideways and it flew over the fence and into the woods. No big deal. We climbed over the chain-link fence, retrieved the ball, and continued our game. We spent the remainder of the day playing, cooking out, and having fun. It was a good day. We returned to my aunt's home with an uneventful evening and I went to bed.

I awoke in the morning feeling quite itchy and had red bumps on my face, hands, arms, and legs. It was familiar to me because I had something similar before. I showed my aunt, and we concluded that I had gotten into the poison sumac that was relevant in the woods behind her sister's house. She got me Benadryl and calamine lotion, and I preceded to become a tired, itchy kid covered in pink goo. The only problem was it didn't get better. It got much worse. I developed large bubbles full of fluid all over my body. The bubbles covered my arms, legs, torso, and my face so badly that much of them, predominantly the ones on my face, I had scratched so badly that I had developed scabs. My right eye had swollen shut, and I only had a sliver of my left eye open so I could see. I was miserable. I couldn't sleep well. Taking a bath burned. It was bad. So

> **My right eye had swollen shut, and I only had a sliver of my left eye open so I could see.**

bad in fact that when my mom returned home from her trip, she passed me by in the driveway because I was unrecognizable. She looked right at me yet could not tell under all the bumps, blisters, scabs, and calamine lotion that I was her daughter! Of course, after I spoke up, she realized—to her horror, I'm sure—that I was her daughter. She gasped then hugged me tight and preceded to ask me and my aunt what had happened. We explained. Then we packed up all our stuff, loaded the car, and started the one-hour drive back to our home.

During the trip home my mom asked if I had prayed and asked God to help. Of course, I had prayed! Prayed for it to go away, prayed that the itching stop, prayed, prayed, prayed! Then Mom told me about a lesson on tape she and my uncle had listed to on the drive back from Florida. It was a lesson about the power of healing. In that lesson, the man spoke about how we are children of God and how Jesus came to not only die for our sins, but how he was also beaten and by his stripes we are healed. Isaiah 53:5 and 1 Peter 2:21–25 are a few among many scripture verses quoted. As children of God, not only can we pray and ask for healing, but it is our God-given right to CLAIM that healing in Jesus name because it had already been done for us. So my mom said we were going to pray and CLAIM in Jesus name my healing. That is exactly what we did. The remainder of the trip home was spent talking about our week, her week, and so on.

> **So my mom said we were going to pray and CLAIM in Jesus name my healing. That is exactly what we did.**

Once we arrived home, we unpacked the car and got everything situated at home. My mom asked me to go wash the calamine lotion from my face and arms in the bathroom sink and said she would put fresh lotion on. I complied. I remember standing in front of the bathroom sink, like I had done several times during that week, waiting for the sink to fill and examining my face. At least the best I could see out of one half of an opened eye, I looked horrific. I had scratched scabs so badly that I knew I would have scars. My face was the worst of my body.

Now don't get me wrong, the rest of my body was bad too, but my face was the worst. The sink finished filling up, and I added soap. I proceeded to wash the stinky pink lotion from my face. I rinsed the soap off when I was done washing and reached for the towel that hung next to the sink with my eyes tightly shut and dried my face. I opened my eyes, hung the towel, and looked in the mirror to ensure I got all the lotion off. I let out a scream that made my mom come barreling into the bathroom as she was sure something was wrong. From behind me I heard my mom ask in panic, "What's wrong?" I turned to her in disbelief. The scars were gone! The bumps and sores were gone! Both of my eyes were wide open! It was all gone! In that very instant as I washed the lotion from my face, it was like I had washed away all the poison sumac and its effects. Not only on my face, but my whole body was healed. I was in shock. Our prayers had worked! All I could say to my mom was "It's gone, it's all gone!" My mom simply looked at me and replied with a smile, "What else did you expect?"

It always put me in awe, that in this ever-changing world where nothing stays the same, things change on a dime, and people tend to change their minds as often as we change our clothes, God is always the same. Never changing, a constant (Numbers 23:19 and Hebrews 13:8). Even when we stray or exercise the free will he gives us, his promises for us stay the same, even through the years.

When I was about sixteen, I was very active in church. I went to a private Christian high school that our church ran. We were there every time the doors were open. Even when they were not opened to the public, we were there because my mom cleaned the church for extra money, and we helped. I was also part of our youth group and don't recall missing a meeting. I remember one specific youth meeting where our youth group pastor spoke about how God gives you the desires of your heart (Psalm 20:4). She said she interpreted that to mean that God places certain desires in your heart that follow his plans for your life. Such as being attracted to certain qualities in a person, so you will be drawn to the man or woman he has designed for you. She went on to say that we were reaching dating age,

> I remember one specific youth meeting where our youth group pastor spoke about how God gives you the desires of your heart.

and it was possible that we could soon meet the person God designed for us and we would marry. So we were given a task. We were to go home and create a list. It could be as specific or as vague as we felt led. A list of all the qualities we wanted in our "perfect" mate. We could even get as specific as eye color, shoe size, hair color, et cetera. Then when we started dating someone whom we thought we might marry, we could go back and check our list. If they checked EVERYTHING off our list, we would know that the person was the one God meant for us. She said to make sure and pray and to ask God for guidance in making our choices.

So I went home, walked into my room, and shut the door. I set out to do the task I was assigned. I started out praying and talking to God about what to put on my list. The longer I prayed, the more I felt like making a list of specific items I wanted in the man I wanted to spend my life with was too restrictive. It was for me anyway. I did not want to put God in a box and get so detailed. So I had a conversation with the Lord. I told him the qualities I wanted in the man I wanted to marry were obvious. I wanted him to be kind, love the Lord, be a good father... you know, obvious people wants. I wanted him to love me like crazy, beyond understanding. That ooey-gooey, sickening kind of love that you see in movies. In fact, there was a Brian Adams song that was, and is, one of my favorite songs, the one from that movie. The song "Everything I Do, I Do It for You." I told God that THAT was the way I wanted the man he made for me to love me. So I told God that would be the way I would know who the one for me was. "The man that you made for me, God, would play me that song. That's how I would know."

Now, as I stated when I began this story, God gives us free will. That's what sets us apart from other beings. The ability to make our own decisions and not be told or dictated on what we must do. He also has a plan, a perfect will for each of our lives (Jeremiah 29:11 and Hebrews 10:36). We don't always fall into his perfect will, because we choose to walk his path or the one, we want. No other reason, it's simply all about our choices. That does not mean that it is the one designed by our heavenly Father.

With that being said, I did make my own choices and married prior to my husband. It ended, obviously, and that is another story for another time. I always remembered that prayer and that covenant I made with the Lord that day about the man I wanted to marry, but I didn't follow it myself. Many times, in the moment, we think we know what is best for ourselves. Or not even that, but what we want in that moment, or at that moment in time. Free will allows for those choices and those decisions. That's what makes up human beings.

During my time of being single, I recall a day of being out and about, driving around and running errands. During that time, I had a conversation with the Lord, as I would many times in the car by myself, about that prayer. So much time had passed since I had made that pact with God and that song was so old. It never got played on the radio anymore and you didn't hear of it anymore. So maybe, because of that, I needed to change my song. Pick a different one. Update my pact with him. In a small subtle voice, I heard, "I do not change. I am constant. Although time has passed, my promise remains the same." With that, I ended my prayer, and went on about my day.

> **In a small subtle voice, I heard, "I do not change, I am constant. Although time has passed, my promise remains the same."**

When I met the man who is now my husband, we were friends for several years before we began to date. When we began to date, I knew. I knew he was the man I wanted to spend the rest of my life with, and he said he felt the same way. The timing was not right for us. He broke off the relationship, and for some time, we did not speak. I was hurt and shocked and made sure there was distance between us. Fast-forward a year or so, he came back into my life. He began by apologizing for hurting me and wanted to be friends. I was reluctant because of the past hurt and on prior attempts of him contacting me, I had not responded. This attempt, I felt something had changed, and so, cautiously, I began talking to him again. I kept him at arm's length for a while to see what was different. He and I have spoken about it since then, and he said that he knew. He wanted to take things slowly, at my pace so I would know that this time things would be different.

After a while we began to date again. We went to church together and spent time with one another. One night we were at my apartment, sitting at the kitchen table. We were going through YouTube and Facebook and such. Watching funny videos, listening to songs, enjoying each other's company. During that moment, he spoke up and said, "Oh, there is a song I have been meaning to play for you." He pressed Play on the YouTube video, and the Brian Adams song from my childhood, the one I made my pact with the Lord about, began to play from his phone! I immediately threw my hand over my open mouth, and tears began to flow. I'm not just talking a tear or two! With everything I am, I began crying in joy. Here he was, the man God made for me, sitting in front of me, playing that song!

> "Oh, there is a song I have been meaning to play for you."

God's promise had come to pass! In that moment, I would forever know that he was the one I was meant to be with! Now you can imagine my husband's panic as I began to weep! He thought he had done something wrong. *Oh, my goodness, I made her cry!* He immediately shut the video off and began apologizing—for what, he had no clue. I asked him to keep playing it, but he didn't want to. "You're crying, why would I do that!" I tried to compose myself and asked, if I explained, would he play it again? He said "Maybe." I began to explain how when I was just sixteen years old, so many years earlier, I had a conversation with God about him! As they say, the rest is history.

In life, so many things have happened, good and bad. This fast-paced, crazy world we live in will always change. It will always evolve. Good, bad, or indifferent—that's the way it is. But it's good to know that God is the same today as he was yesterday, and he will be the same tomorrow as he was in the beginning. Healing still happens, promises are kept, because he is God. Today, tomorrow, and forever. For that, I am forever grateful. For it's hard to find a constant in this ever-changing life.

> https://www.youtube.com/watch?v=vFD2gu007dc
>
> Bryan Adams, "(Everything I Do) I Do It for You" LIVE—SPECIAL EDIT, Feb. 21, 2009

STORY 31

Terri Black

I GUESS I'VE ALWAYS had a relationship with God. When I was very little, I took all my problems to him. He always answered. Of course, in my youth I always listened for him. I remember one time when I had a tough decision to make between two different dolls, and of course I went, sat on the steps, and prayed really hard about it. I was there speaking to God for a while when my dad opened the door and said, "There you are! I should have known you were praying. It's raining on either side of our property, but not on our house."

> "There you are! I should have known you were praying. It's raining on either side of our property, but not on our house."

God gave me a terrific gift of being able to see my guardian angel. He, my guardian whom I named George, would stand in our bedroom doorway every night to keep watch over me, my sister, and my brother. If any of us woke with nightmares, he would tuck us back in and rub our legs until we fell back asleep. Now as I've grown, my guardian has kept an eye on me still, and my children. When times are tough, he is more visible.

When I was at one of my lowest points, God got me through it. When I was told I wasn't good enough, that I needed to stay in the situation that I found myself in, God said I was enough. He had someone out there who would appreciate me. He kept showing me this man who would sit in church with me, with no complaining! This man wore a flannel shirt, jeans, and work boots. I thought, *Who wears work boots to church?*

As the years passed, God would remind me of this man, letting me know the man wasn't ready yet. Well, neither was I. Many years passed before I was ready to change my situation. I was very scared. God let me know that I wasn't alone. He lined up a job (actually, two) and a place to rent.

My job turned out to be the best thing for me. I now have a wonderful work family. I know I was placed there for a reason. With this job, plus my other part-time job, I was able to support myself, which I was told repeatedly that I could not do. I worked two part-time jobs for over two years before I got full time at the newer job. When he knew I was ready to start a new relationship, he pushed me out of my darkness. He had the perfect guy ready for me. He always gives me choices, and in this case, I listened to him.

I had told him years ago what I wanted and needed in a partner. I truly believe God was working us toward each other for years. This wonderful man wears flannels, jeans, and work boots to church! He has his own relationship with God and treats me with respect. It really was love at first sight. We are keeping God first in our relationship, another first for me.

I see God working with me every day. I just have to remember to be still and listen. I am learning not to worry or fret about things like I use to. God has it. It feels great when I let go and trust God has it. It's all in his time not mine.

STORY 32

Don Kister

IN 1969, AT the age of seventeen, I was working a part-time job at a cola company in Wooster, Ohio. I would go to work every day after I got out of school. I was a junior in high school at the time, and my job was as a forklift operator.

Back in the day, there were no protection shields on the forklifts. I would regularly lift pallets of cola bottles in cartons onto high level shelves above the ground. One day while operating the forklift, I had one carton of cola fall on my head, knocking me out. I was taken to the Wooster Community Hospital first and then was transported to Canton Hospital, where I was in a coma for days.

While in my room, I had an out-of-body experience. I was above everybody looking down. I tried to talk to everyone in the room, but nobody was able to hear me. I saw my mom, dad, sister, brother-in-law, my brother, and my girlfriend.

> **While in my room, I had an outer body experience. I was above everybody looking down.**

I then went through a tunnel of bright light. I became very calm and at peace with myself and wanted to continue through the light. I was stopped by a figure in front of me. I believed it was Jesus. He told me it was not my time yet. He told me to go back and be with my family. As I was coming back through the tunnel of bright light, I entered my room again. Looking down on my family, I saw the priest sitting beside my bed.

I finally woke up from my coma. I had to wait until the nurse took the tube out of my throat before I could speak. I asked the priest what he was doing there in my room. He said that he was there to read me my last rites. I guess the nurses told my family to say their goodbyes to me before the priest read me my last rites.

To everyone's surprise, I lived that day, and that was over fifty years ago. That is exactly what happened. It changed my life and perspective. Many lessons were learned throughout the years, but the most powerful memory was when I was seventeen years old and hearing Jesus say, "It's not your time yet."

STORY 33

Jessica and Madison Pritt

MY NAME IS Jessica Pritt. I am twenty-seven years old. God has truly given me a miracle. Our story starts when I found out I was pregnant as a senior in high school at eighteen years old. I was due December 28, 2010. I grew to love my baby more and more with each passing day. My mother was a huge supporter, after she forgave me for my lack of responsibility. She felt the baby was a gift from God.

My mom was out of remission and back to battling stage 4 multiple myeloma. She was scared she'd never get a chance to be a grandmother. She was so passionate about this little miracle. She made it a priority to look for the baby's heartbeat every night before we would go to bed, sometimes during the day when she couldn't wait until night. She would sing to my belly and talk to my belly. My mom, Cindy, was so excited to be a grammy. She went to every baby appointment alongside me.

In August 2010, at about nineteen to twenty weeks' gestation, we were at my appointment to finally find out the gender of my baby. Little did we know what struggles we would have to endure to get where we are today. At that appointment, I was told how PERFECT my baby GIRL was looking and was congratulated for becoming a mommy to her. It was a happy time. Mom and I celebrated by going to a local baby store to pick out her first outfit ever. We also had chosen a talking stuffed monkey and Madison's first ever pair of walking shoes.

> **The first thing the next morning, I had received a call that shattered my whole world.**

The first thing the next morning, I had received a call that shattered my whole world. That dreaded phone call was the doctor telling me there were alarming issues with my ultrasound. Those issues were that my baby had edema (major swelling) on her neck, hands, and feet. And that I had to go to Akron Children's Fetal Medicine as soon as possible.

The words "AS SOON AS POSSIBLE" haunted me all the way there. Through tears, I prayed constantly, "God, please let it be a mistake on the doctors' end! Please let it be nothing as serious as they think it is. Please, God, give me the chance to be the mother I know I can be to my little girl."

Mom held my hand every step of the way. As soon as I walked into the room with the doctor, I was told my baby girl had a possibility of having Turner syndrome. We shortly found out the doctor didn't have high hopes of her survival at all. She kept saying my baby, which I just found out the day before was a girl, was going to die in my womb.

The doctor then started to push me to abort, even after I made it very clear that I would never even consider abortion. She still was constantly trying to pound it in my head. She stated that if she could say 100 percent that MY baby was going to die, she would.

I was very, very upset. Mom stepped in and put her foot down and told this doctor that we were NOT going to abort and that it was out of the question. She said, "It is all in God's hands."

After this disagreement with the doctor, I was told that I HAD to have an amniocentesis. The whole time the needle was inside my womb with my baby girl, I could only stare at my mom as she was making sure the doctor didn't try to harm my baby on the monitor. After all this, our next stop was the cardiologist right across the hall.

You can imagine how I was after the conversation with the last doctor. I couldn't stop crying. My insides hurt and my heart was so broken. I was so lost. So I prayed. "God, please let this be good news. Please give me hope that she will be OK." I walked into that office, where I met Dr. Patel. In all these past years of specialists after specialists, Dr. Patel has been the most influential.

He asked me why I was so upset. So I told him about the doctor right before him. He told me to never lose faith, and that he was going to look at my baby girl's heart. As Dr. Patel evaluated the heart of my baby girl, he found that she did in fact have two heart defects: a coarctation of the aorta and a partial anomalous pulmonary venous connection. Thankfully, both can be corrected through surgery. Dr. Patel also said that my baby does not have any hydrops (excessive fluid along her heart and/or lungs). He stated that he didn't understand why the previous doctor said what she said because if my baby did not develop hydrops, we had a better chance at being able to hold my living baby girl.

God gave me hope. Meeting Dr. Patel and receiving his news was my hope. We had to see the cardiologist once a week to make sure my baby never developed hydrops and that she remained stable.

> **God gave me hope. Meeting Dr. Patel and receiving his news was my hope.**

The result of the amniocentesis did in fact confirm my baby girl had Turner syndrome. This is a rare chromosomal condition affecting only 1 in 2,500 females who are missing or partially missing the X chromosome. Most fetuses conceived having Turner syndrome (approximately 98%) will spontaneously miscarry during pregnancy. Only 2 percent of TS fetuses survive to term. My baby is part of that 2 percent. There are two different types of TS: one is classical Turner syndrome (when a complete whole X of the XX is missing) and mosaic Turner syndrome (when the abnormalities only occur in some of the X chromosomes of the body's cells). My daughter was diagnosed with mosaic TS.

Girls with Turner syndrome are at higher risk of developing many health issues—including but not limited to heart and kidney abnormalities, hypothyroidism, ear infections/hearing loss, and growth issues resulting in growth hormone therapy. Since my amniocentesis was confirmed, we were able to do our research and prepare for whatever God had planned for me and my baby. I had weekly doctor visits to check in on how she was doing. After all, God let my little miracle be a part of that 2%.

On October 8, I was admitted to the hospital because I was not gaining weight. This meant my baby girl, Madison, was not gaining or growing either. I had to be on a baby heart monitor 24-7 to make sure she was OK. This had to happen until Madison was here.

Every morning, I had one wheelchair ride to my ultrasound where they gave Madison a test to make sure she was doing OK inside me. If she passed the nonstress test, we were good. Other than that one wheelchair ride each morning that I spent with my mom or dad, I was on strict bed rest with her on the heart monitors 24-7. There were nights where her heart rate would decel (drop to scary lows due to a compressed umbilical cord or because her blood flow decreased). I would have to be turned on my side or be given oxygen. During all that, Madison would be given the nonstress test. Luckily, every time it happened, we were able to get her heart rate back up to the safe baseline.

After many visits with my mom, dad, sisters, and brother along with many friends and family, the day finally came. On November 15, the ultrasound showed I needed to deliver immediately. I was told that I needed to have an emergency c-section. I was terrified!

I wasn't expecting it was time for her to come into this world, let alone have the doctor who told me to abort her be the one on call. I refused to let her be the one to deliver my daughter. Thankfully, there was another doctor available. The doctors wanted her to be at least six pounds. This was because Dr. Patel was prepared to do open heart surgery on her as soon as she arrived, although she was nowhere near that weight.

I was prepped and cut open. The doctor pulled out my baby girl, who was not crying or moving. She was taken to another room where I finally heard her cry minutes later. I was so scared, especially since I couldn't hold her or see her. They needed to get her ready for transport to Akron Children's.

> **Madison was in the NICU for 43 days, I was with her every single day. When she was in her incubator, I was alongside her doing my schoolwork.**

The first time I was able to finally lay my impatient worried eyes on my daughter was right before they transported her. I felt so helpless. I had to hold on to that amount of love that I felt in the very moment, since I was not able to hold her or stay with her. Once they took my daughter, we realized I was having an allergic reaction to the epidural. Every part of me wanted to be with my baby girl. I didn't care about what condition I was in, I only wanted to be there for her. I was told I had to wait at least eight hours, which was forever to me. They had given me medication for my allergic reaction which knocked me out. Once I was awake, I had to prove to them that I was stable enough to go to the other hospital to hold my daughter.

The time finally came where I could hold and see my newborn. They did not have to do open heart surgery right away like they assumed. She was born at three pounds, fifteen ounces and 16½ inches long. Her heart defects were still there, but fortunately, the coarctation of the aorta was not restricting her blood flow to her heart. GOD IS GOOD! God gave me my baby girl! He gave me my chance at being her mother. He was there through every hurdle, showing me that she is a fighter, and that I am worthy of her.

Madison was in the NICU for forty-three days, I was with her every single day. When she was in her incubator, I was alongside her, doing my schoolwork. She had complications such as jaundice and had a hard time latching on to any nipple. Madison needed to be fed by a feeding tube through her nose and had terrible reflux, which prevented her from keeping milk down.

She also had MRIs and many tests done to make sure the issues she had would be properly addressed in due time. One of the tests showed she had a tethered spinal cord, but in order to do the surgery, they wanted her a little bigger. The doctor said if I were to decide that the procedure would not be done, her spinal cord could snap like a rubber band and leave her paralyzed from the waist down for the rest of her life. So I had big decisions to make.

In order for me to take her home, she had to get a G-tube. This looks like a button where I had to connect tubing to feed her and a Nissen. A Nissen is a procedure where they tied her stomach in a knot to avoid reflux. This allowed me to feed her once she left the hospital and for her be able to keep it down.

She had her first Christmas in the NICU. Three days later, we were able to take her home. A few months after that she had surgery on her spinal cord. In May 2011, I graduated with honors, holding my daughter. With every struggle we had, God and my mom showed me that I was not alone.

We lost my mom in August of 2012 due to cancer. It was just shy of Madison's second birthday. I needed God more than I ever did. God knew I would need my daughter after losing my very best friend. God knew what I needed before I needed it. When I lost my mom, half of me died with her. Madison and I were so lost without her. She didn't understand, which made it harder on me. To this day Madison asks about her grammy, as she was Grammy's girl. She has such a huge heart and a great memory to remember that inseparable bond they had shared. We talk about her often.

All we can do now is take things day by day, month by month, and obstacle after obstacle. With the constant support from my family and friends, especially my nana, we get through the hardest days. Leaving what comes next in God's hands, letting him guide us to where we need to be.

Madison fought so hard when all the odds were against her. She is eight years old now, fighting everything that comes at her with no struggle. She's my superhero and has had over twenty surgeries with others coming in the future.

Madison is the light of my life and the one who keeps me together. The person she has become has been such a joy! She is very outgoing! Madison's heart is so pure and big. She reminds me constantly that God loves us, and without him, we would not have gotten this far. As we are still waiting for our break from her surgeries, we are blessed to have her here. God has truly given me a miracle, and I will be forever grateful.

STORY 34

Lynnette Fowler

MY STORY DOES not involve a healing but rather an instance when my son wanted to die. God sent a miracle in the form of a marine recruiter. He arrived at the perfect moment to my son's front door and pulled him out of the depths of despair.

My son is only seventeen years old. He and his dad have not had a lot of contact until these past three years. He is graduating this year and is freaking out a little about his future.

There was a particular day in which he had just reached the end of his rope. We were on the phone, and he said, "Why don't you just let me die?" This broke my heart.

The conversation just went downhill from there—fast. Finally, we hung up, and I started praying. I was asking God to send his ministering angels to comfort and minister peace and comfort to my son. When we were on the phone, I had asked him to go talk with my cousin, Mark. He unequivocally said, "NO!" So I was also believing that God would change his mind and he would agree to talk to Mark. It was less than thirty minutes later when I received a call from him. He said, "I'm sorry, Mom. I'll go talk to Mark."

> **It was amazing! I saw God move in a powerful and miraculous way that day.**

My son has been preparing to go into the marines, and that particular day, the recruiters were going to stop by the house to talk to him. Well, after we hung up, I texted the head recruiter. I explained to him that it probably was not a good day for them to stop by. However, the second in command did not get the message, and he showed up at my son's door. All he had to do was grab my son and give him a tight hug, and that turned the tide. It turns out that recruiter was an angel in disguise sent by God to be Jesus in the flesh as he hugged my son. My son's human angel let him know that he was in no way forgotten by God.

It was amazing! I saw God move in a powerful and miraculous way that day. I give God all the glory! My son went from wanting to die to feeling he belonged and had a purpose. As a mother, this was my miracle and the answer to my prayers.

STORY 35

Trang Le

Every Twist and Turn in Our Lives Are the Ways God Leads Us to Where We Are Today

IT WAS THE last part of April of 1975. The air was getting warmer, sprinkled with a few showers here and there. Despite all that, and as young as I was, I could still feel the heaviness in the air around us. My parents would use their hush-hush voice whenever I entered the room. As tense as it was around me, I was oblivious and just went on to enjoy that little piece left of my childhood in my country, Vietnam. Many events happened in a short period for my young mind to digest.

I remember vividly, like it was yesterday. It was around mid-morning, my family was among the crowd of panicking people who, for one reason or another, needed to get out of Saigon. There were six of us kids and two adults. My dad was holding on to one son in one hand, and my other brother in the other hand. As the oldest child, I was holding one brother's hand. My mom, who was pregnant, was also holding my two sisters, one in each hand. My youngest sister was only two so, occasionally, my mom would have to carry her.

The crowd would rush toward any landing planes. The planes would hesitate to even land, as people would be on the tarmac waiting to get on any landing plane. It was pure chaos! People from behind us were rushing and pushing. They separated

> **They separated us, the family, a few times. We always managed to get the family back together.**

us, the family, a few times. We always managed to get the family back together. And the chaos continued. One lady who appeared to have come from behind us, offered to hold on to one of my brothers for my dad, who would then be able to help my pregnant mother with my youngest sister.

My mom and dad thought it was a great idea. The lady was taking hold of my youngest brother. A few more pushes from the crowd, and the lady plus my brother were separated from us. I still remember the pure paralyzing fear sweeping across my being. My first thought was we would lose him for good. In this condition where the crowd could separate anyone, losing a family member is as real as the sky is blue. As those thoughts were going through my mind, I heard my mom scream, "Where is Quan?" (Quan is my brother's name.) My dad must have realized it at the same time. In panic, he told us to hurry up and follow him. As we were scanning the crowd for the lady, we did not realize there was a plane that managed to land near by us.

My dad immediately was looking at the plane and saw the ladder had been placed by its door. The lady and my brother were among the people on the top of the ladder. My dad left my mom in charge of the kids and ran toward the ladder. He was pushing people aside as he was approaching the ladder. His action was met with violence, as everybody was trying to get on the plane. He had to explain to everybody around him why he needed to get to the top of the ladder. After a few more minutes of struggling with the crowd, he was able to get to the top of the ladder and retrieve my brother. My brother was oblivious of the separation but was glad to see his dad. They left the ladder.

On the ground, my mom was crying, and so was I and my other sister, who was old enough to understand. We could have lost him forever had we not realized soon enough the lady was separated from us.

So you see, I truly am convinced, "Every twist and turn in our life is the way God is trying to lead us to a safe destination." I can't really credit anyone but God for the safe return of my brother. Because of that incident, we value family and each other more than anything. We literally had experienced the saying, "Your loved one can be ripped away from you at any time."

STORY 36

Ward Edinger

MY NAME IS Ward E. Edinger. I have told my story many times when someone would say something to question if God is real. I had an experience in May of 2004. While driving my van to take someone to a cancer treatment, before I arrived at their house, I had severe chest pains. Then, everything went brown and white. I felt like I was separated from my body yet telling my body what to do.

I told myself to slow down and pull to the side of the road and stop. Then I said, "God, I need your help on this one." No sooner than saying that, the pain went away; normal colors came back, and I felt normal. I went back home and called the doctor's office and told the nurse what happened. She told me to get to the emergency room immediately.

> **No sooner than saying that, the pain went away; normal colors came back, and I felt normal.**

I made a couple of other calls to let people know what was going on and drove to the hospital. The next morning, I had a stress test, and the results were not good. I was Life-Flighted to Akron General Hospital. The next morning, Dr. Tobias found 70 percent blockage in a main blood vessel, and two stents were put in end to end.

I was told by the doctor, if the clot that hit the blockage had not passed through, I would have died. So I know from personal experience that GOD answers a call for help.

STORY 37

Chris Smith

ON NOVEMBER 18, 2017, I woke up in the hospital. My ex-wife told me what had happened to me. My brain was bleeding, and they had to get me to OSU fast. I couldn't talk and was told that I had a stroke.

When they were taking me upstairs, I somewhat had my wits about me, but I couldn't talk. I could not believe what was about to happen. "What! I was about to fly in a helicopter?" Those who know me well know I am very fearful of flying. The weather was bad, however, and they couldn't fly me. They therefore had taken me by ambulance to OSU Emergency Room. I remember the whole ride there. And that was when I heard his voice telling me, "Everything is going be all right." Whose voice? some would ask. I'd say it was God.

The thing about me is, I find humor in every situation. I find humor in myself, and, that is how it has always been for me my whole life. I can't change things. So I have to laugh! I make the best of my situation. I feel Jesus was telling me about myself and my strength when he told me, "Everything is going be all right." I believe what Jesus spoke to me is a part of me now. I know "everything is going to be all right." I continue to do my best in life, and he continues to guide me through my life.

> **The thing about me is, I find humor in every situation.**

When I was in the hospital, I was with a lot of stroke patients. I could see people half my age wanting to quit. I wrote a note to them, encouraging them not to quit! "It's about you and your strength" is what I would tell them. I tried my hardest when I was there in rehab. I did everything I could do to help myself improve, and I supported others in doing the same.

After I got outside the hospital, things were a little tougher. I certainly had struggles. But then, I heard it again, "Everything is going to be all right." Every situation I came across that was tough, I just powered on through it like a running back. Even when I would come across negative people, I would tell them, "It's going to be all right." When they didn't agree, I said, "OK, you will see." Even when I had a breakdown, I prayed, thanking God, "Everything is going to be all right." He kept telling me, so I kept trying.

Speech therapy was hard. I once was well-spoken, but suddenly, it was gone. I know the therapy helped to get some of my speech back and for that, I am grateful.

My cousin said something to me a few months back. What he said, has stuck with me and always will. He said, "When we were in your hospital room, everyone looked worried except for you." I didn't know back then but I know now that God had me, and it wasn't my time to go yet. I do know this, without him, I wouldn't have made it!

It's been over a year now, and I'm back to living my life again. I have a new house, and I drive. I have a wonderful job and work for an amazing woman, Amanda Ratliff. God gave me another chance at my life. I hope in the end, I did all right.

STORY 38

Afton Hill

NOVEMBER 16, 2016, while doing a bit of grocery shopping along with my three boys, I received a frantic phone call. The call was from a telephone number that I did not recognize, asking if I knew my fiancé at the time (now my husband). I advised the caller that yes, I knew him, and she began to tell me that she was a nurse calling from the hospital where he had been flown to and that he had been involved in a severe accident.

At that very moment, my life stood still. I had so many questions. Was he on his motorcycle? If so, was he wearing his helmet? My biggest question of all was, is he going to survive this accident? The nurse advised me that the accident involved another vehicle hitting his SUV where he was ejected from his SUV. She then took a long deep breath and began to update me with his injuries and advised that there were no promises that he would make it.

Upon my arrival at the hospital, I spoke with the doctors. They informed me of the multitude of his injuries and how unlikely it was for him to survive. They stated that they had patients with just one of his injuries and did not survive.

> **At that very moment, my life stood still.**

I can remember speaking with my mother, who was also there with me at the hospital, and we began to pray. I remember my mother telling me not to receive anything that the doctors and nurses were telling me. "Do not let it manifest in your spirit." I did just what my mother advised me to do, by blocking all negative thoughts and self-doubt. We were told that he suffered a severed kidney, severed spleen, severed pancreas, severed aorta, retinal hemorrhage, fractured vertebrae, and broken ribs.

We went through months of him being in a coma. He was on a respirator and feeding tube, and he had a tracheotomy. We continued to pray and asked the Lord for healing over his body, and I began to cry out to the Lord. I pleaded with him, stating I was unable to raise these two-, three-, and twelve-year-old boys on my own. After countless attempts of trying to take him off the respirator, one day his body was FINALLY well enough to breathe on its own. He was transferred from the ICU to a step-down unit, to a rehabilitation facility. While traveling back and forth to and from the hospital to check on my husband, my health also began to decline both physically and mentally.

My life at this point consisted of fighting with insurance companies, hospitals, doctors' offices, and his family members. They were upset with me because I wanted him to receive blood to save his life, and it was against their religious views. While facing these battles, Hurricane Irma hit Jacksonville on September 10, 2017, with a vengeance. This hurricane forced my family and me out of our apartment. We lived in a hotel in Georgia for months where I drove daily back and forth to Jacksonville, making sure my kids remained on track in school. One day while riding around in search for a new place to stay, we noticed a sign in a yard and contacted the realtor. She showed us several properties, but everyone turned us down. We were then blessed to be introduced to a private owner who was willing to give us a chance despite our circumstances. We now had a place to call home again.

The accident left my husband disabled, where he has to remain under the care of various specialist for the remainder of his life. Taking care of the boys along with my duties to care for my spouse makes it quite challenging to work at times. I was so blessed to find a job as a network development consultant. The people I work with are a blessing. I'm not even sure if they know how happy I am to be a part of such wonderful spirits and such a great company as a whole. The purpose of the job is also so fulfilling because I know I am helping someone, which I believe is my purpose in life.

Everything in life has seemed to fall in place through divine intervention. I know for a fact that it is only the Lord that has been keeping me and my family together. I thank him for all that he has done and is doing in our lives. I look back and reflect on a few years ago and just begin thanking the Lord for his wonderful works.

STORY 39

Kathy Weitzel Christian

MY NAME IS Kathy Weitzel Christian. My story begins in a small town where everybody knew everybody. My parents were godly people. I was raised in an Ozzie-and-Harriet environment. Dad worked full time, and Mom was a stay-at-home mom. My mom played the organ at our Congregational church, and all of us kids were in the choir and youth group. We couldn't have asked for better role models as parents.

At the age of fourteen, a friend of mine asked me to come to church with her, so I did. This was a Baptist church that she went to. That was the day I was saved. What a new outlook on life I had from that moment on. I encouraged the rest of my family to become born again. Thank God they all accepted Jesus as their Lord and Savior. I know we will all be in heaven for eternity.

In my senior year of high school, I met my husband at a high school dance a friend took me to. It was love at first sight (in my eyes). I didn't know then that we wouldn't see each other again until a few years later. When we did see each other again, it was in God's time. We were married a year later. Little did I know how hard the last name would be to live up to.

> **That was the day I was saved. What a new outlook on life I had from that moment on.**

We were both raised in different environments. Me being the third child of godly parents, and him being the oldest of eight boys being raised the best they could by parents who weren't Christian or didn't hold to a faith-based model. My rose-colored glasses of the perfect "happily ever after" were soon broken. I strived to be a good example of a Christian woman to his family. I would show them love, kindness, and patience. It would be God's timing that they would come to know the Lord. Praise God for the ones who have made that decision to accept Jesus Christ as their savior and choose to follow his ways. We are still praying and working on the ones who haven't yet.

We raised two children the best we knew how. God helped us guide them to him. Like many parents who were raised in different environments, it was sometimes a struggle, but God won out every time. We now have two wonderful grandsons we help guide to seek his wisdom in all their life struggles and accomplishments.

My life has had many ups and downs. God has been there through it all with me. I praise him for both because I have learned things from them. AMEN!

STORY 40

Marty Lotito

THE NUMBER FORTY is an interesting number. As I sit here praying for God to give me the ability to best share my story, I am six months away from my fortieth birthday. It has been seven months since a moment happened in my life that I will never forget.

September 10, 2018, began like most Mondays, rushing out the door. As Danielle (my amazing wife of thirteen years) and I got our daughters, Lakyn (nine years old) and London (seven years old), ready for school, we began another busy start to the week. Around lunchtime I spoke to my mother Rosemary and father Tony, as my mother was getting ready to go to her cardiologist for her checkup. She had recently been diagnosed with congestive heart failure. The doctors truly cared for her and were working on a treatment plan to best manage her care. I told my parents to, "Keep me posted on what the doctor says, and I will call you all again later in the evening."

Later that same afternoon, after I had just come home from work and had picked up our daughters from their elementary school, I saw a text message come in from my sister Katie saying, "Mom is unconscious. EMS is on the way." I stared down at my phone for a minute, not really comprehending the weight of that moment. A few hours earlier, I had just talked to my mother on the phone. As a believer in the Lord, and knowing how fragile our human condition is and how we are citizens of heaven and earth is just a temporary moment, I still had to brace my emotions as I started to uncontrollably tear up.

Immediately, I walked outside my home to my front yard. My little girls were inside playing, and I dialed the landline to the home where my parents had lived for almost fifty years. I knew something was wrong when my father first picked up the phone. I could hear it in his voice. He was giving my mother CPR and telling me, "She's gone . . . she's gone." Up until this moment, I had never heard my father cry. Not that there is anything wrong with crying, but he just never showed those emotions. He was a true "man's man," who loved the Lord and always worked hard for his family. He taught me so much wisdom. I asked my father to put the phone up to my mother's ear. My mother loved the Lord, and I prayed for Jesus to take her home. At this point, she was already in heaven at the age of seventy-one. I remembered how, three days earlier, she had left me a very unexpected voicemail on my phone that really caught me off guard.

After I hung up the phone, I called my wife and broke down on the phone with her, telling her to come home as soon as possible, as she was working late that day. My wife has been there for me through many difficult times. Her faith in the Lord is strong, and I knew I would need to lean on her in that moment. When my wife pulled into our garage, I immediately lost it and had not yet told our girls what had happened. We said a prayer together and walked back into the house and told our girls that Grandmommy was in heaven. Our sweet girls, who thankfully know Jesus at such a young age, knew that Grandmommy could walk again, and they would see her again one day in heaven.

> **After I hung up the phone, I called my wife and broke down on the phone with her, telling her to come home as soon as possible, as she was working late that day.**

Back in July, our girls had seen how tough it was for my mother to get around at our annual summer family trip to Myrtle Beach, South Carolina. It was crushing for me to see her not able to walk when we played miniature golf. It was sad when we asked if she wanted to go out to Broadway at the Beach, and she said she would not be able to go because she could barely get around. That was the first time I could ever remember that she did not go with us. It was difficult for our girls to see this. My mother loved to get out and go places with her granddaughters, and I could tell how much not being able to get around truly disappointed her.

After I told my girls the difficult news, I gathered my emotions and walked up the stairs in my house. I turned on Christian radio and heard one of my favorite Christian songs, "Do It Again." I knew God was speaking to me and that everything would be OK. I went on to pack my bag and left my house in Nashville to drive to Knoxville to pick up my sister. We then began the almost six-hour drive from my house to where my parents lived in Virginia. My sister and I laughed and cried together as we thought back to all the memories we had with our mother over the years. We drove up the familiar road to my parent's house and got there around 3:00 a.m. I parked the car and gathered the courage it took to take those emotional steps down the driveway and sidewalk leading up to the front door. I walked into my childhood home and went downstairs. I saw my mother's empty Diet Dr. Pepper can on the table beside the chair where she would always sit. I saw her reading glasses and opened book of crossword puzzles, her oversized pocketbook on the floor that she would always take with her everywhere. But she was not there.

I then saw my father sitting in his chair, bent over crying. I went toward him, and that is when the emotion of that moment hit me like a ton of bricks. We knew my mother was in heaven, but they were married for over fifty years, and just like that, my father was now alone.

Through that pain and in that moment, God showed me his love and grace. A lady from our church had so kindly stayed with my father until we arrived so late into the night. That is when God told me, "This is what health care should look like." Truly caring for people when they need our help the most was what God showed me. I felt like God was showing me how we should be more involved in our faith communities and local churches to help improve our broken health care system.

That previous Saturday night before my mother went to heaven, she had left me a short voicemail. My mother, who never complained, said, "I just feel so weak, and your father is doing such a wonderful job taking care of me. Don't be afraid. I love you." That next Sunday morning, when I checked my voicemails, I immediately called to make sure she was OK. She sounded fine, but in hindsight, it was as if the Holy Spirit was telling her to get ready for her journey home.

God was so faithful through this pain, as he had also given me one last earthly moment with my mother. My cousin had a wedding earlier in August in Cincinnati. We all attended, and I was able to dance with my mother and see her one last time. A funny thing happened as the wedding reception came to a close and my family and I were beginning to leave to make the long drive back to Nashville later that evening. As I told everyone goodbye, I saw my mother and father standing near the exit door and went up to them and gave them both a hug and told them I loved them, and as I looked back the Lord spoke to me, "This is the last time on earth you will see your mother."

> **God was so faithful through this pain, as he had also given me one last earthly moment with my mother.**

I shrugged it off and did not pay it much attention, except when I walked out the door and looked back one last time at my mother and father. It appeared to be as if I was looking at her through a narrow tunnel, and that moment of her smiling and waving goodbye back at me, was frozen in time. I did not share that experience with anyone until after she went to heaven. It has made me more aware of what the Holy Spirit is doing in my life on a daily basis and how I need to be more intentionally aware of his presence.

My prayer and hope is for whoever may be reading this, learn to live in the moment. Learn to see the good despite what you may be going through. The pain we endure on earth is only for a moment compared to the eternal glory of heaven. Slow down, unplug, be kind to others, make time for your family and loved ones, because you never know when that earthly moment God gives you will be your last.

STORY 41

Joe Carfelli

Comfort in the Ashes

I HAVE BEEN A fire Investigator for a very busy medium-sized city in Northeast Ohio for over eighteen years. Before that, I was a firefighter/paramedic. During that time, I saw the best and the worst in people. I have seen people, including children, who have died in fires. I have seen children brutally murdered by a parent. I have seen shootings and stabbings. I have also witnessed the saving grace of God in many lives, including my own. And I have seen people comforted by seemingly inexplicable findings during times of personal tragedy. As all first responders know, we often meet people on the worst day of their life. As an investigator, I often have extended contact with them both during and after the incident.

> **I have also witnessed the saving grace of God in many lives, including my own.**

I had shown the picture of the Twenty-Third Psalm from the story below to a friend of mine who in turn shared it with LuAnn Topovski. When she asked me to write it out for this book, I did just that, nothing more. That story, though inspirational in and of itself, is just part of a bigger picture. I was talking to my sister about the Psalm 23 story, and she said, "Wow! I just got goosebumps. That's just like when we found Dad's picture." That brought back a wave of emotion, and I couldn't believe I had not made the connection before.

In 2010 our father died from injuries sustained in a gas explosion in his home. Without going into too much detail of the cause, he had an accident the night before that left a small nick in his gas line to his stove. The gas seeped out all night, filling the house. He called me that morning asking if I would take him to get a new stove after work. Within an hour or so, his house exploded with such force that it knocked the house off its foundation. The ensuing fire destroyed nearly everything in the house. It is a testament to his strength and the grace of God that he was able to get out of the house. Though he succumbed to his injuries the next day, he was able to talk to me prior to being transported to Akron. He was also able to communicate with family and friends who prayed with him for hours that day. He indicated by raising his hand that he accepted the gift of eternal salvation through Jesus Christ before he passed away the next day.

Sometime that following week, after the house was released to the family, my sisters and I were digging through the debris, trying to salvage anything that remained. It was pretty disheartening, and more than a few tears were shed when we would find something of particular sentimental value which was now scorched or melted. Gone were the photo albums, scrapbooks, paintings that Dad had painted, sports memorabilia, etc. We then picked up a crusty bundle from where his scrapbook was, and as we pulled it apart, there was a large picture of our dad. He was young, smiling, and in his prime. What a comfort it was to find this picture. No other picture from that book would have had the same impact. Perhaps this is why when I'm digging out a fire to determine the cause, I keep my eye out for something that could bring comfort to the family.

> **We then picked up a crusty bundle from where his scrapbook was, and as we pulled it apart, there was a large picture of our dad.**

I think of 2 Corinthians 1:3–4 NIV, "Praise be to the God and the Father of our Lord Jesus Christ, the Father of compassion and the God of all comfort, who comforts us in all our troubles, so that we can comfort those in any trouble with the comfort we ourselves receive from God."

I investigated a fire that we believed a young boy set a couch on fire while playing with a lighter. His sister woke the father, who was taking a nap in another room and he got her and the other kids out of the house, but they could not find the son. After the fire was extinguished, his body was found behind a door in an upstairs bedroom. Everything in the room was completely burned from top to bottom, with the only unburned carpet being under the body. The family, of course, was in anguish. In that room, inexplicably untouched by the fire, was this young boy's baseball mitt. It was taken to the family sometime later. It was my hope that they were comforted with this personal item of their son's.

Another fatal fire I was lead investigator on was a fire which occurred between Christmas and New Year's, where five people lost their lives. One of them was a twelve-year-old visiting his mother's house for Christmas. He lived primarily with his father in another town, so most of his personal belongings were at that home. This house was completely burned and collapsed into the basement. There was nearly nothing salvageable in the debris except for a knife in a metal case that I understand was a Christmas gift. It was not a particularly expensive knife. It was one you might find at a truck stop with a favorite NASCAR driver on it. In this fire, there was melted metal from the extremely high temperatures, but this knife and the box it came in were untouched.

A few years ago, I was sent to an address in North East Canton, Ohio. I was to investigate the cause of a house fire. It is an area of modest homes, mostly two- to three-bedroom bungalows. Many homes were occupied by retired factory workers from the nearby industrial area.

I was met on my arrival by the battalion chief, who filled me in on what they had observed so far. He stated that when the firefighters pulled up, there were flames and heavy smoke rolling out of the windows, and that an older couple was standing outside with a small dog. The couple told them that everyone and all pets were safely out. The fire was quickly extinguished, but the fire had already gutted the house.

I spoke with the couple outside. The husband, though visibly shaken, was trying to be strong and console his wife who was sobbing and said something about losing memories of the past forty years spent in that house. They asked if I could attempt to find their car keys and if it would be possible for them to go in and see how much damage there was.

When I first entered, everything was blackened and dark. It's what we term as a "black-out." I noticed a bright white spot across the room as I moved closer. I could tell it was a framed embroidered Twenty-Third Psalm, with the glass broken out around the verse. It had broken out perfectly and in perfect timing from the cool suppression water hitting the heated glass. It broke out around the verse and fell out of the frame when the smoke had dispersed enough to leave the now exposed embroidery a stark white. I photographed the verse and continued with my work, though I couldn't quit thinking about it.

It took me about an hour to complete my origin and cause investigation. I located the car keys and then accompanied the couple in to survey the damage. The husband stood there looking around while the wife moved from one object to another, crying softly and making remarks about something else lost. She then looked across the room and saw the white spot, almost glowing in stark contrast to the black surroundings.

> **"Everything is going to be all right."**

She walked slowly toward it. She reached out and ran her hand across the embroidered verse as she read it. She then turned to her husband, smiled, and said, "Everything is going to be all right." She quit looking around at the damage, took her husband by the hand and left the house.

I didn't get much opportunity to speak with them after that day. I dealt with their insurance company some and learned they decided not to move back into the house and had instead moved down to Minerva to be closer to their daughter and grandchildren.

This incident made such an impact on me. I carry the picture in my Bible to remind me of that impact as well as the peace that God can give someone in a time of great adversity.

Perhaps this fire was God's way of releasing this couple from the trappings

of years of accumulating "things" and making it easier for them to move closer to family.

Most recently, holy relics were rescued from a roaring fire at Notre Dame Cathedral, including a crown of thorns believed to be the actual one placed on Christ's head, and a large crucifix was found unburned in the debris. I was not there and don't pretend to know the extent of the fire in the area where these things were found, but it seems amazing that a crown of thorns could survive a fire.

These are just a few examples of how God, even during times of great tribulation, sends a Comforter, which is the Holy Spirit, to comfort us during times of loss and trouble.

Joe's Dad, Jim Carfelli

STORY 42

Joshua Bechtel

Give yourself
The grace to acknowledge your losses
And grieve them
And experience the range
Of emotions,
Your hand in the loss,
And others' hands in the loss.
Allow yourself
To pick through the rubble
And sift through the debris.
It is true that there has been devastating loss.
It is also true that there is usable material
In and amongst
The debris and rubble
Of the brokenness.
You CAN reuse this salvageable material.
You CAN restore and rebuild.
You CAN replace ashes with beauty.
You CAN create beauty out of ashes.
You CAN rebuild
What has been destroyed
And has been lying in ruins
And has been dormant
For many generations.
You CAN do this.
It is your inheritance.

> It is your heritage.
> It is your destiny.
> You CAN
> (And you WILL)
> Rise up
> And build.
>
> —Joshua Bechtel

I WAS NOT BORN a Bechtel. I was not even supposed to be born Joshua Paul. I am not sure if I was even supposed to have been born, meaning I do not know if an abortion was considered on that day in November 1977. I am told that I was supposed to be born Terry David. You could say that nothing about my life has been the way it was supposed to.

My parents were not even married to each other. They were somewhat crazed, irresponsible hippies of the seventies. He was an already divorced Vietnam War veteran. She was wild, somewhat crazy, red-headed Debbie.

My first taste of travel was before I was born. Circumstances forced Terry and Debbie to hitchhike from Detroit, Michigan, to Pendleton, Oregon, in August of 1977. I was born on November 4, 1977. I am told my mom almost died and my dad unsuccessfully slit his wrists on the day I was born. My biological mom, instead of naming me after my dad, named me Joshua Paul.

I was born with a touch of fatalism that was not entirely my fault. Being moved around to four foster homes before the age of eight did not help the touch of fatalism. This inner fatalism was not helped by the fact that I was eventually adopted by conservative Mennonites who lived in a tiny logging town of Estacada, Oregon.

One day in school, one of the vocabulary words was *illegitimate*. The definition made my young blood run ice-cold right there in the classroom: "someone who was born to parents who were not married to each other." And that is the moment what was left of my self-confidence crumbled into ashes.

I survived school. I joined church. I got a reasonably decent but boring job at a nearby nursery. This job became my full-time job when I graduated from high school in 1996. I was nineteen.

Once in a while I house-sat for my boss and his family when they were on vacation. It was the week of Thanksgiving. Mom had been hammering the idea to me that I needed to forgive my biological mom. I was perfectly miserable. Wednesday evening after prayer meeting, our chorus practiced for several upcoming Christmas appointments the next month.

Mom and Dad went home right after prayer meeting.

We got through prayer meeting and chorus practice, and my brother gave me a lift to the nursery, which was just up the road from home. We pulled in and parked by the gate. My brother turned off the ignition, and we sat there in the dark. We talked for a long time about a lot of things. This was a powerful turning point in my life.

I felt as if I was standing in front of a stone wall. God stood right there as well, saying "It's up to you, buddy. If you refuse to forgive your mom, your walk with me is over."

What are you supposed to do when God says that to you? What can you do but give in? Finally, after several hours of unendurable spiritual warfare, I was given the grace to utter the words, "OK, God, I forgive my biological mom."

> **"OK, God, I forgive my biological mom."**

When I said those words, I felt like I had become a new person. I felt as if I had finally tasted what it was like to be born again. I felt like I had let go of everything that defined my life up to that point. I had "let go of the rope" and had every sensation of free-falling. The next day was Thanksgiving.

In the following weeks, I faced a huge problem. How was I supposed to contact my mom? I tried to draft a letter—about a page is all I got written. Suddenly, I felt blocked.

Then, I thought, or heard from God, "Get her phone number and call her."

Gulp. OK.

After several calls and one or more dead ends, I got what was supposed to be my mom's phone number. A day or two before Christmas, I made the call. My biological mom said it made her day and her Christmas.

Meanwhile, I was scrambling to pack and get ready to leave for Virginia. I left home in Oregon that January and worked at the children's home for several years, from 2001 through June 2004. In the course of those years, I did several stints of night duty. During one round of night duty, the almost incredible happened.

It was in the middle of a night duty stint that stretched to nineteen nights, in the late winter of 2003 or early spring of 2004. I was folding laundry in the downstairs laundry room. Thinking my own thoughts . . . if I was thinking at all. It was approximately midnight.

I heard a voice.

"It is time to go look up your real mom."

I wondered if the length of time I was on night duty was affecting my head. The next night, same time. Same place. Doing the same thing. "It is time to look up your real mom." I was almost convinced I was going crazy. I put it out of my mind, again. The third night. The same place. Same time. The same words. "It is time to go look up your real mom."

As I stood down there in the laundry room, my heart began pounding hard. My mind began racing. Maybe this was for real. God had just told me to go look up my real mom.

Several months later, I made the trip out to Oregon and met her. Over the course of the next couple of years, I would go out to visit her at least three times. She passed away within two years of our first meeting. I will always say that God gave me the two-year window.

> **Several months later, I made the trip out to Oregon and met her.**

I eventually met my biological dad. Too many overlapping and interconnected things happened in the next several years to relate here. I concluded my term at the children's home and applied to work at a men's rehab center in Indiana. I eventually worked close to seven years at the rehab.

I eventually left the rehab, and to a number of the staff there, it probably looked like I had lost my grip on reality and life and faith and God. I probably had, come to think of it.

For a number of months, I did not attend church anywhere. I felt like I was more or less led into a wilderness. Part of that wilderness included having it out with only God and myself.

I am not sure if I would recommend doing this to just anyone. However, it might be healthy once in a while. It helps to get away from systems, religion, and all that is involved in church. It helped me find where I stood on my own two feet.

After the experiences of the previous year or so, I needed to do just that. So I sort of allowed myself to drop off the map for almost a whole summer. I pretty much just existed in or around Arcola, Illinois. Around August, I came back around and told a friend of mine (neither of us were attending church anywhere at the time) "I don't know about you, but I need to fellowship with somebody . . . somewhere."

I knew of some ex-Amish families who were meeting as a small group up the road from where I lived. One weekend, almost spur of the moment, I decided to "break my church fast" and meet with these folks who met in the basement of one of their houses. By the time the service was over, I knew I had found the group God wanted me to fellowship with.

Several months later, someone mentioned a couple of the girls in our group were going to get baptized in a couple of weeks. My heart skipped a beat. I asked if I would be able to be baptized also. So it was arranged.

> **My heart skipped a beat. I asked if I would be able to be baptized also. So it was arranged.**

I had come to Arcola in what must have looked like insane obedience. I had obeyed the illogical looking nudge to get immersed. And I knew it meant severing some more Mennonite ties. Meanwhile, I had been doing some serious study on the baptism of the Holy Spirit. And I was plodding through some intense personal issues of my own.

I would read and then try to pray. Sometimes I would be able to pray through and get a sense of release in some areas. But I seemed to be blocked. I knew what I wanted. I had longed for it desperately . . . but it seemed just out of reach. It was almost as if someone was trying to keep me from receiving the next thing God had for me. It would take the arrival of a frankly unpopular preacher who would come with a foundation-shaking series of meetings at a nearby Mennonite church.

The week of Good Friday saw a number of tornado watches come through the area. There was also a spiritual earthquake, and it came in the form of a preacher named Wayne. He preached night after night from the altar at the foot of the pulpit because God told him to, in order to break down any spiritual resistance that had built up as a result of years of preaching the wisdom of man and tradition that denied the power of God.

One night there was a tornado warning. And for several nights, people in the audience were healed of various illnesses. Then came Good Friday.

It was a gloomy, cloudy morning, even for the area. By eleven o'clock in the morning, it still looked like early morning or twilight. When I awoke that morning, I was in such physical pain that I could barely get out of bed. I have frequently had severe migraine headaches, and I thought that was happening. I finally was able to get up, and we went to the laundromat to do laundry bachelor style.

Meanwhile, my head—every part of my body, actually—was throbbing. I felt light-headed, and it was all I could do to stand upright, let alone have a conversation with anyone. The slightest noise was enough to almost drive me out of my mind. We went across town to get a bite to eat, and I managed to keep down some food.

That afternoon, there was going to be a meeting for anyone who was interested to join in a time of sharing, fellowship, or whatever would occur. My friend decided to go, and I was riding on the strength of pain relievers at that point. So I decided to stay at the house and try to regain my strength so I would be able to go to the evening service.

Since I was not there, I am not going to try to say what all happened in that meeting. I will say, the Holy Spirit powerfully showed up. Meanwhile, approximately three in the afternoon, I started to feel well enough to get up and get a shower and slowly get ready to go to the meeting.

The thought crossed my mind. "What if something happens over at the church this afternoon and you aren't there to see it? Will you be able to believe it is from me, and will you be able to accept that it happened without you being there?" I knew it was God asking those questions. The words of Jesus flashed into my mind. "Blessed are those who have not seen and yet have believed" (John 20:29 NIV). "Yes, Father," I said, somewhat mystified.

At about six I got a text from my friend: "The Holy Spirit visited us." I was totally unprepared for what I saw that evening in the meeting. I could barely comprehend the change that had come over my friend. There was every evidence that it was real . . . and I was honestly afraid of what I saw. The service eventually ended. We all went home.

My friend and I sat in the car. He was talking full speed ahead about what had happened that afternoon and what was happening in him even then. When there was a pause in what he was saying, I turned to him and said, "Do you have any idea how long I have waited to see something like this?"

"No," he said, "I probably don't. You have probably waited and wanted it longer than most of the rest of us." After a while we got out of the car and went into the house. My friend began doing what he called spiritual house-cleaning.

I went into my room in sort of a daze. To be honest, I was jealous, just a little bit. I knew I had told God I was fine with not being on hand when the others had received the visitation of the Spirit. But I wanted it in the worst way. With a pounding heart, I went over to the living room where my friend was sitting and said, "OK, I'm ready."

> **"OK, I'm ready."**

Before long I was face down on the floor. At first the words would not come. Then I began praying and repenting and confessing attitudes and sins of the spirit that I did not even know were there. That night their presence and power loomed large.

After several agonizing moments, I was able to utter the words, "God, I forgive you for all the crap that I have blamed you for causing in my life." This opened the gates of my spirit, and I began to pray and forgive yet again a long string of people. As the Spirit brought names and faces to mind, I said, "Yes, I forgive them . . . and them . . . and them . . ." I prayed in this manner, going extremely deep into a lot of painful areas. Until we hit a roadblock.

The scene at my adoptive dad's bedside came into my mind unbidden. (I was crying uncontrollably by this time.) Still face down, on the floor, I envisioned myself at the Father's feet. "God, did I make all that stuff up . . . about Dad?" I was sobbing uncontrollably and pounding the floor with my fists as I asked this. "If I made it up, load me up with condemnation or something. I need to know."

Somewhere along the line I asked . . . begged . . . demanded the Spirit. I was more desperate than I had ever remembered being in my life. I lay on my face for several minutes, waiting for what would come. The only way I know to describe it is that a sad peace came over me. I sensed the Father telling me, "We both know you didn't make it up. All the things you have remembered, they have been true." He had one other word for me. "But I was there, all the time, even when you didn't know it."

About this time, I began feeling what I can only describe as a hot tingling sensation starting in my hands and gradually going all through me. "God, I don't know if this is the baptism of the Holy Spirit or not, whatever this is that is coming on me. But if it is, give it to me, and I will accept it." I felt myself immediately engulfed in the power of the Spirit and love of God.

I felt my mouth begin moving and making words that I did not understand. It began as a bit of a dribble. But then suddenly . . . I knew I had received the "sign gift" of tongues. I did not know until a few days later that it was more than simply a temporary, one-time gift. My friend said later that I appeared to him to be in a sort of trance, although I was totally aware of what was going on around me. According to my friend, I kept on speaking, or praying, in tongues for over an hour. At one point, my friend said, "God, you are giving him a language to speak to you directly from his spirit. And I will not speak against it."

When I heard him say that, what was going on "clicked" inside my mind. Even so, I found myself wondering if I was making this all up. I attempted to form English words. But it was as if the Father said,

"Nope, you aren't going to talk English until I let you." The conversation in tongues, with God, lasted apparently over an hour. I am sure my spirit and the Spirit of God had some dealings about some deep-seated things.

> **At one point, all at once, I began laughing . . . as if my spirit had attained a measure of release and freedom.**

At one point, all at once, I began laughing . . . as if my spirit had attained a measure of release and freedom. I finally got up off the floor and went to my room, my mouth still bypassing my natural understanding and conversing with God in tongues. I looked over at my friend and motioned that I would talk like normal if I could, but I couldn't.

Finally (it was around two in the morning by this time), it began to subside. I was "given" the English language back. The first English words out of my mouth were a long string of "Thank you, thank you, thank you, thank you." Several evenings later, it occurred to me that I HAD been given an actual prayer language. I could use it to talk to the Father, direct.

So I wrote the following praise poem:

Father of my Lord Jesus Christ,
Thank you for this
Incredible,
Supernatural, unexplainable
Gift of your Spirit.
You have given me a language to speak directly to you
In the Spirit.
You have given . . .
And promised . . .
The ability to interpret
What you have given me to say in the Spirit as well.
Thanks, and glory be to you.

STORY 43

Christy Jackson

IT WAS MONDAY morning, June 2, 2015. I was sitting at the kitchen table, drinking my coffee and paying bills. It was a typical Monday morning as some may have. It was the first few days of summer break, and the kids were excited to enjoy their summer, taking advantage of their free time playing.

Then time stops and races all at the same time. From one room away, I hear the tone of a scream that no parent wants to hear and the sound and sight everyone begs never to see. The images my mind stores away are ever so fresh, vivid, and left me a bit different. Some people go into panic mode, freeze mode, or work mode. I found my two-year-old daughter (Attlie) drawn up in a fetal position, lying on her back, eyes rolled back, blue and purple—not breathing.

I heard the screams from my ten-year-old daughter begging my name, "Mommy!" My mind raced to calculate the situation. What has happened? How could this happen? I was literally three feet away in the next room! Attlie (two years old) and Avery (ten years old) were playing quietly in their room. Is she having a seizure? How is her body so stiff and drawn up? How is she so blue so quickly? None of this makes sense!

Every second felt like eternity. Time was racing, yet it felt like time stopped. My life as I knew it and had planned for literally stopped. I started picturing and feeling the immediate emptiness, pain, and unknown. Is this how it's going to be? *Such a short time with her, Lord. Why? How? No, LORD! Please, NO!*

I found myself and my ten-year-old daughter screaming, praying, begging out loud. "No, Lord! NO, LORD! Please give her breath, LORD. Give her life, Lord." Pleading with him that he doesn't take her now. My head was screaming. My heart was screaming. My soul was pleading. All this simultaneously as I picked her up to give her CPR. I immediately started giving her chest compressions and then breathed into her mouth. Nothing happened. I was rotating from chest compressions and giving her breaths. Begging, pleading, "God, please send your breath from heaven and make her breathe!"

> **My head was screaming.**
> **My heart was screaming.**
> **My soul was pleading.**

My mind was racing. Seeing her eyes rolled up in her head and her body blue was horrifying. Was she choking on something? I'm screaming for the boys Wyatt and Wade to get my phone as they stand in the doorway in pure fear and chaos. I'm telling Avery to call 911 on my cell phone. Avery's mind was simply frozen. She was just yelling out to God to help her. I realized she couldn't call 911. I laid my phone down on the floor and dialed 911. I'm frantically trying to pry Attlie's mouth open to see if I could see what she was choking on. Her jaw was clenched tight. I could barely get her mouth apart to see anything, but nothing there. I tried to reach my finger to the back of her mouth, and she clenched down on my finger so tightly I could not pull it out from her teeth as 911 answered and heard the hysteria.

Avery was crying out; I was now screaming because Attlie is biting through my finger, and I was trying to give our address. I stated that I had found my two-year-old daughter not breathing and unresponsive and that I desperately needed them to get to my house.

I had no idea what it sounded like on the other end of that operators' line. All I knew was that I was instinctively trying to make my daughter breathe, I was crying out to God, "Please don't' take her!" I knew our life as we knew it was in the balances. It felt like everything I was trying was not working, no matter how hard I was trying. I couldn't get her to take a breath. I was starting to feel helpless. My mind was already sorting through the idea that if this was the Lord's will, then I must trust him. If this was his plan, then he will help me through this, imagining her taken away from us too soon. Feeling the sadness of not having enough time. All this while I'm still working on her to take a breath. Chest compressions, breathing into her, begging it to make her not lifeless.

I had to rip my finger from out of her mouth. Her body had settled from stiff and rigid to flat, and her eyes stopped rolling back. Her body had calmed, and her eyes were open. Is she breathing? Is this it? Everything was calm and quiet, yet it really wasn't. There was a deep quiet and almost like a pause or stop in time (really, probably my mind drowning out the commotion). She said, "MOMMA." She knew my name! She could talk. She was here!

> **she said, "MOMMA." She knew my name!**

She was pale white; her color was different than when I found her, and she acted very sleepy, like I was waking her from a deep sleep. My mind amazingly started to wonder how much damage was done while she was not getting oxygen to her brain and body parts. *Will she be able to walk? Will we have to start over again? Or will it be fine? She is alive! And she said, "Momma!"*

All the while, I did not know that the boys ran down our long driveway and waved down the ambulance. The boys let them into our blanket-fort-ridden living room to the bedroom we were in. I was able to tell them she had just taken a breath and said, "Momma." They began their evaluation and took her temperature. They said she must have had a febrile seizure (yet she did not have a high temperature). I knew in my heart this was no response to a fever. I was so very thankful they were there and that they said she was stable. But they needed to transport her to the hospital for further evaluation. My gut said not to let them take her. As crazy as that sounds—and yes, they were not very happy with me for thinking that—I knew she needed to get to Cincinnati Children's and not our local hospital. In the next few minutes, it felt like I signed my life away in the back of their ambulance, as I signed to decline their treatment and recommendation for transport.

I called my mother-in-law and said I needed her to come and stay with the kids while I took Attlie to the hospital, and that I needed her soon. I didn't want to overalarm her, but I think she knew in my voice I needed her. I called my husband Steve and told him he needed to come home from work and it needed to be now. I never had to do that, as he was self-employed, and thankfully, we could make that happen right away.

Within the next hours ahead, we drove an hour to Cincinnati Children's, and with the weirdest, most stunning drive. I was quiet, solemn, and yet, matter of fact in telling Steve what had happened. There were seriously no words to describe those minutes that felt like eternity and a race all at the same time.

We spent the next several hours in the Children's emergency room telling them what happened. She stopped breathing and I had to give CPR to bring her back. She had just turned two years old two days ago; we had a small party for her at church the day before, and she didn't really want to eat her cake. I thought that was so weird—what two-year-old didn't want to eat her cake? Later that Sunday night, she just wasn't acting right, but nothing really stood out. I thought, *Well, maybe she's coming down with something.* The next morning (Monday) I was supposed to go to work, but she still wasn't herself. She was acting kind of punkish, quiet, and just off. She normally goes to a babysitter friend's house. But that day there was eleven other little ones, and I decided I better call off work.

Calling off is something I would rarely do. I hated to do it because it inconvenienced my coworkers. I was dependable, and calling off wasn't really an option for me. But I didn't know if she was coming down with something, and if she was, it wouldn't be considerate of me to send her to the sitter and get the others sick.

It was our first Monday out of school, and the kids were just playing. Around ten o'clock that morning, I was changing Attlie's diaper and noticed her lips were a different color, a purplish color. I thought, *Are they always this color? Oh, I'm just overthinking things. Maybe they are this color, and I just haven't noticed.* I told the hospital the timeline of the past two days and that at approximately ten thirty that morning, she stopped breathing. They proceeded with bloodwork, full physical, and EKG. Her temperature was normal; her heart rate was a bit lower than normal, but otherwise everything had checked out fine. They too felt like she was fighting some kind of virus and maybe had a febrile seizure. They gave us a number to follow up

My mind was trying to make sense of all of this as it really did not make sense.

with the next day for a neurologist. They discharged us and sent us on our way.

We went home and Attlie did just fine the rest of the day. She could walk, she could talk—we had our girl! My mind was trying to make sense of all this, as it really did not make sense. I had been a veterinary technician for the past thirteen years. I was familiar with seizures. They are awful to watch. I was used to piecing information together to figure out what was going on. Although Attlie was not completely herself the hours before her event, she did not fit the story of "unknown" seizure.

Seizures don't make one stop breathing and turn blue and lifeless. It felt like bringing home a newborn baby all over again watching every breath, keeping my eyes glued on her. Was she really in the clear? Whatever happened, would it happen again? That night she of course slept in our room, and I couldn't sleep for fear it would happen again and I wouldn't know. She slept well through the night and never did get sick. She had no fever and was just fine.

In the morning, I was changing her diaper, and I noticed her lips again. This time I knew I wasn't crazy. This was not her normal color. Again they were a blueish purple. I thought I would call to follow up with the neurologist and let them know she still had the discolored lips. When I called the nurse, they thought I was calling from a message from the cardiology department. I said no, I was supposed to follow up with neurology. I was actually in town running errands to get caught up from my previous day. The nurse said they wanted to run a couple tests and if I could bring her back now. Not that it was an emergency but that if I could get there in a couple hours and that I might pack a bag for overnight in case they need to keep her.

I thought that was a bit strange, and I told her I needed to make arrangements for our three other children and then I would get down there. Steve and I went back down to the hospital that afternoon. They admitted her to the cardiology department for more testing and that the doctor on the previous night shift wanted to look further. The cardiologist that worked the night shift goes over every EKG from the day shift, and he also happened to be the head of the cardiology department. They decided to keep us overnight for observation since they still wanted to run additional test based on the previous events from the past two days. On Wednesday, they just watched her and told us that we might want to go home and get some things packed because we might need to stay longer.

Attlie was doing great and just hanging out with Mom and Dad, and she had us all to herself. We had much bonding time over those quiet days—something that we normally didn't have in our busy life of work. Thursday came, and we were waiting for our daily rounds and test results from the previous past two days. I remember Steve going down to the cafeteria to get a snack in the afternoon. It was all quiet, and Attlie was taking a nap. I was just sitting there in a chair facing the window, noticing it was sunny out.

These days had been a weird quiet, calm, and peace as odd as that sounds. A few doctors asked to come in and speak with me. They introduced themselves and that they wanted to discuss some of their results and plans. Again, time kind of went silent, tingly, alone, taking in all the information as I struggled to wrap my head around what all this means for our Attlie and for our family. My first thought was she might not be able to be a mother and experience that gift. Maybe no man would want her for a wife, as he might likely lose her in their marriage and might not want to know that pain ahead of time.

My initial thought was, *Are you serious? Heart surgery? You mean we can't fix her? There's something badly wrong with her heart, and we never knew it?* They were serious, and I couldn't figure out how all this could be. I never in a million years had this in our story, any of this.

I took this all in calmly and quietly and wished they would have waited until Steve was with me to tell me all this. As they were describing their past few days behind the scenes, Steve came in, and they proceeded to tell us that on Monday night, Dr. Knilans, head of cardiology read Attlie's EKG. He noticed something that he recognized while reading in a textbook years ago yet had never seen before. Something so rare that you only read in textbooks as most patients do not survive past the cardiac event. He wanted to do more follow-up tests to confirm his thoughts and diagnostics to be sure. He said that Attlie had short QT syndrome, which affects the electrical function of our hearts.

Our hearts have a mathematical pattern of 0.00035 on a scale correlated to the letters QRST. This mathematical pattern keeps our hearts beating at a regulated beat pattern. Attlie's is consistently 0.00029, which is shorter than the .00035 (short QT). If our pattern is more or less, our heart stops. There are only seventy documented cases, and this was the first time seen at Cincinnati Children's. Statistics show that less than 6 percent survive this cardiac event. In this case, we were told, the precautionary EKG was normal and saved her life.

> **They said that indeed her heart did stop that Monday morning and that CPR saved her life and that all of this is beyond rare.**

They said there is no cure for this and there is no treatment. They said that indeed her heart did stop that Monday morning and that CPR saved her life and that all this is beyond rare. They gently unfolded their plans on how they felt best would save Attlie's life from that point on. That was to install an ICD (intracardio defibrillator). This was to ensure that if and when Attlie's heart should stop again, the ICD should give her a shock treatment to get her heart going again. That this was no guarantee, but it was their best option at this time.

They were so gentle while telling us all this. They told us that she truly was a miracle. They told us she was scheduled for surgery as soon as they could get an opening. They even commented on how well we were doing with all this and that they were in awe. Many tests, consults, wires and teams were our life for the next several days. Attlie never did lose her spirit while going along with all the doctors needed to do.

We spent eleven days in Cincinnati Children's. Surgery took about seven hours. They had to split open her chest and rib cage to expose her heart. They implanted the ICD in her abdominal wall and ran wires up to her heart. It's literally like a battery and backup generator. The battery will last approximately eight years, and we will have to replace it with another surgery. She will need the ICD for the rest of her life.

Recovery—seeing her body limp and unresponsive again—was tough. She was pale, with tubes and wires coming from everywhere, and I saw her new battle mark (huge incisions down and across her body).

However, I like to think of it as her victory line. Attlie recovered quickly, and within forty-eight hours postsurgery, they were set to send us home! This was the most surreal feeling that they literally were telling us to go home and live our life. They said, "If you don't, you will worry yourself to death. Treat her like any other two-year-old," they said. It was eleven days of a pause button, an immediate halt to our lives, lots of hours of time of reflection, peace, an eerie calm.

Yes, is was terrifying to see our baby taken out of our arms for surgery, seeing her in recovery, and the whole process to this day leaves us in awe. It's as fresh as yesterday. I don't talk much about it because it's too hard to take my mind back there to relive it, yet I am in daily amazement and have indescribable gratefulness. The entire orchestration is nothing but unexplainable. God's hand in this is undeniable. That's just God, and that's how he works. The fact that something told me to call off work that day (something I rarely would do), to the fact that had she gone to the sitter that day, she would have been with eleven other kids. Who knows how that would have turned out? To the fact that we took her straight to Children's and not the local hospital like EMS wanted, to the fact that the head of the cardiology team, Dr. Knilans, worked a night shift that night and saw her EKG. That we landed in the exact hands in the right time in the right place. That's God! That when I was giving her CPR and I was trying with all that I had in me and it was not working, and my mind was frantically scrambling inside that I could not get her to breathe. I was begging for his decision to intervene, to change his mind and let her stay here on earth with us, and she finally took a breath, looked up, and finally said "Momma." That's God!

I have no idea of the whats, the whys, and the hows. But what I do know is what I saw and what I experienced was God's plan, love, and provision that later felt like security, peace, and a weird calm. Something unnatural. Something supernatural. Something chosen. And I don't know why he chose Attlie or our family. But I am grateful my children literally saw God move and work before their eyes. It felt as an undeserved humbleness, but that without a doubt, it was HIM.

He was that close to me, yet I couldn't see him. He heard my internal screaming prayers. He came down from heaven to be with us, to breathe life before our very eyes. That he chose us, and we don't know why, but he did. There was just an unexplainable type of peace and presence throughout those eleven days. Our family, I think, was a bit wigged out. They said we had a weird ere calm about us, and I remember agreeing with them that it wasn't us, that it was God. To this day, four years later, we are still in awe of his closeness. The reality is, he is everywhere.

We can look at anything and see his love, protection, and provisions. Our family is nothing special; we are not heroes. We are just thankful, grateful, and humbled at his ways. I would be doing no service to him if we didn't share his ways. We read multiple accounts from the Bible of his miracles. I think it is easy to think he only did those things then, but he is as much alive today as he was then. He still works and he still hears. He promises he would never leave us nor forsake us. I cling to that promise many days.

> We are just thankful, grateful and humbled at his ways. I would be doing no service to him if we didn't share his ways.

I write this to share and give him all the glory for all our days. Not because he truly moved before my eyes, I didn't need that drastic of a move to believe in him, but maybe someone is on the fence about believing if he is real. Is he true; is he faithful?

I never doubted that there was God. When I was a kid, we did not go to church, and I didn't really grow up in a Christian home, but I always believed he was real and prayed to him. It wasn't until later in life (in my twenties) that after Steve and I were married, did I hear the words *saved* or *salvation*. I didn't realize it was a decision I needed to make. I thought I was a good person, I believed in him, and that was my way to heaven. I didn't know it was about knowing what Jesus did for me. No one had ever told me that a sinless man died for me, that he took my sins (all my sins) to the cross and paid my debt. This was my ticket and way to heaven. He did it for free because God loved me so much. Why would someone do that!? I thought that was so undeserved.

At the funeral of my best friends' husband (twenty-two years old), I sat in a pew, watching my best friends heart ripping out. I was hurting so bad for her. While not really hearing the words of the preacher, I did hear that I could make the choice, and have peace knowing I could rest in heaven. I thought, "Who wouldn't want that peace?!" I want to have that knowing peace and assurance. I wanted it settled that day and forever more. I asked Jesus in my heart that day, to forgive me of my sins, and thanked him for dying for me. I had peace knowing I would see my friend again in heaven, as the preacher shared my friend's testimony that he too had asked Jesus in his heart earlier in his life.

That is how I can write this story. When I was pleading with God to give Attlie breath in her lungs, my heart and mind was already calculating the life IF he did not choose that to be his will for our life. I was already trying to find peace and trust in his ways. That I know he holds that big glass globe in his hands. He knows the best for our life, and I have learned to trust him. Not everything in life goes the way we want it or expect.

We are not in control, but when we put our full surrender in trusting in him, life is much easier. It's easier to handle the shut doors, knowing he knew what was down the hall that we couldn't see. When he doesn't answer our prayer right away, when he may even seem silent. It's him orchestrating the path.

Attlie is truly a miracle. We have no earthly explanation or idea what he has for her, but I trust and know he has a plan. I pray you may know and have peace in God's ways, will, shut doors, extreme pain, or emptiness. Call to him, be patient, trust him, no holds barred, give him your heart, and you will rest in HIM.

I pray that if you have not realized you need to be saved, not recognized we are all sinners, or not asked him into your heart and life, you wait not another second. WE are NOT promised another minute on this earth, and many times we want to live in denial. But one guarantee is that we all die. Every minute is closer to our end. The Bible says that we are condemned already. That we are all born sinners (from Adam's sin in the very beginning). But if we humble ourselves, admit we are sinners and ask him to forgive us of our sins, and accept and believe that Christ died on the cross to pay for our sins and the sins of this world, he WILL forgive us, and it will be settled with peace forever. It's as simple as that, all you have to do is pray. It doesn't have to be complicated. You just have to want and mean it in your heart, and nothing can take that away—ever. It's FOREVER.

Thank you for taking the time to read this experience. I give God the glory for all his goodness, even in times of trial, pain, and uncertainty. He is in control. He is peace, and he is unending LOVE. I'm praying for each soul who reads this, and it grows your trust in him.

John 3:16–18
Psalm 27: 14
Proverbs 3:5–6
Hebrews Ch. 11 and 12

Personal photos taken by me and family member.

STORY 44

Pastor Bill Purvis

Dagger to the Heart

> There's a divinity that shapes our ends, Rough-hew them how we will.
> —William Shakespeare

WHEN I WAS growing up in the small town of Eufaula, Alabama, thoughts about the future and faith and God were the furthest things from my mind. I did not have a plan for next week, let alone the rest of my life. And church? I just was not interested. I watched people walk into those buildings carrying Bibles and thought they must all be slow readers. Why did it take them so long to finish one book?

My interests were elsewhere, as in motorcycles and girls—not necessarily in that order. Back in the late sixties and early seventies, you could get your motorcycle license at fourteen in Alabama. I saved my money and bought a Harley-Davidson 250 Sprint. It was my first set of wheels, and I was proud of that thing.

I was the only boy in our family, but I had three older sisters— two who were grown and already out of the house, and one who was three years older and still at home. My father hadn't wanted a boy and had little to do with me. Much later, I learned there was a name for his behavior: the alpha male syndrome. He was jealous and felt threatened by me, afraid I would displace him or somehow take the family's attention away from him. To say my father and I failed to bond would be an understatement.

In my early teens, my father's abusive treatment of my mother left me feeling constantly torn between staying at home to protect her and staying away from home to protect myself. It was a lot of chaos for a kid to endure, but it was my normal, so I did my best to adapt. The male figures I looked up to and tried to emulate were the older boys in my neighborhood and sometimes their fathers. Because our home was so dysfunctional, I often spent nights with friends or camped out with them on weekends. On one of those weekends, one of the boys brought a big ice chest filled with cans of Budweiser.

"If you want to be a man," he said, "this is what you drink." I was thirteen when I tasted my first beer that night.

The following year, a friend's brother came home from Vietnam and introduced my friends and me to marijuana. No one I knew had even heard of it. I was never addicted or a stoner, but I did smoke with friends on weekends. When I was fifteen, an older, married woman seduced me into having sex with her. Once that door was opened, I began having sex with other girls. I'm ashamed to say it now, but if they were interested, you could be sure that I was.

> **Strangely enough, no one seemed to notice or be concerned that I was involved in all these unhealthy activities.**

Strangely enough, no one seemed to notice or be concerned that I was involved in all these unhealthy activities. On the outside, I looked like one of the good kids. In fact, I was so good at keeping up appearances I was twice nominated as a Best-Dressed Student. We weren't poor, so I had enough money to buy all the basics. Plus, our family lived in a new home on Lake Eufaula, and we had a boat docked in our backyard. I was athletic and enjoyed sports. When I applied myself, my grades were mostly As. I also had a lot of friends. As far as anyone could tell, I was a guy who had it all together.

What people couldn't see, however, was the emptiness inside me. I felt aimless. I had no guidance or direction. There wasn't much to do in our small town, so on most weekends I hung out with guys who drank, smoked pot, got into fights, and chased girls. Looking for excitement and adventure, I kept trying new and more reckless things. When a friend threw a cherry bomb through the window of the principal's office, a group of us got suspended. My response was to ride my Harley up the front steps of the school and down a hallway—during class. With the engine noise echoing off the metal lockers, the sound was about ten thousand times louder than I expected. But I was already suspended, so what could they do?

The more I tried stunts like that, however, the less fulfilled I felt. I just had no purpose.

Have you ever felt like that? Or do you feel that way right now? Believe me, I understand what it's like to fool the people around you by pretending everything is great. You also fool yourself, which might work for a while, but it doesn't last. Deep down, you know something isn't right, that something in your life is missing.

All too often, that's how life seems to work, isn't it? Either we're drifting along with no sense of purpose or we're trying to find the answers but getting nowhere. We don't know where we're going, and we don't know why we're here. When we get frustrated and desperate enough, we may try to chart our own course, but we end up in a place that looks nothing like what we had in mind.

That's what happened to me in 1974, the year I was seventeen.

Something's Not Right

My life took two abrupt turns that year. The first was a sudden move to another state. My father started two businesses after he retired from the army: a flooring company and an ice-cream truck operation. They began well but eventually folded. Then he began selling mobile homes and did much better. I didn't know it, but he was in serious debt from the failed businesses, so when the home office for the mobile home company offered him more money if he'd move to Columbus, Georgia, he didn't take long to decide. When I got home from school on a Friday afternoon, my mother was in tears. My father had announced that we were moving from Eufaula to Columbus—the next day. I never even had a chance to say goodbye to my friends. That following Monday, we were in our new town.

The second abrupt turn came on April 28, just a couple of weeks shy of my eighteenth birthday. I'd been cruising the streets of Columbus with a friend in my '69 Camaro late on a Saturday night when I suddenly got an idea. I'd just spotted a young woman standing on a corner. She had long black hair and wore a tight blouse, short black skirt, and high heels.

I turned to my friend. "Danny, you ever been with a prostitute?"

"Nope."

"Me neither. Let's try it."

Danny protested, but I ignored him. I swung the car around and pulled up beside the woman. "What are you doing by yourself on a street corner?" I asked.

"I'm looking for a guy," she said.

"Well, you don't have to look anymore."

As we talked, a man walked up from behind some nearby hedges. He was a couple of inches short of six feet, unshaven, his hair unruly, and had a strong smell of alcohol on his breath. Surprised by his sudden appearance, I briefly wondered if the man was as dangerous as the one he resembled: Lee Harvey Oswald. But I quickly decided that this was "how they do this."

"How much money do y'all have?" the man asked. Between us, Danny and I had about fifty dollars. "All right," the man said. "That'll do."

The man and woman got into the back seat of my car and directed me to a dark, run-down, one-story house in a poor neighborhood. The house sat away from the street on the same lot as a pharmacy. It was long and narrow, with an extra room that had been added to the back. We stopped in the gravel parking lot behind the house, where the woman—I didn't know her name—and I got out. We walked to the house's back door while Danny and the man I thought was her pimp sat in the car.

The back room was small, about eight by ten feet. The only furniture was a wardrobe and a bed. A feeble glow emanated from a single, naked bulb in the ceiling. Across the room was another door that led into the rest of the house.

I locked the doorknob and hooked the chain lock on the back door while the woman appeared to lock the door that led into the house, though I later realized she was unlocking it. I wondered what came next. When the woman began taking off her clothes, I did the same. The woman motioned toward the bed. I sat down.

We'd been in the room just a few minutes when she flipped off the light. I couldn't see a thing.

The floor creaked—strange, since the sound didn't seem to come from where the woman had been standing.

I stood up.

Then I smelled an overpowering stench of alcohol—close—the same odor I'd noticed on the pimp's breath.

Alarm bells rang loud and wild in my head. *Something's not right!*

The light suddenly switched back on. I was initially blinded, but then I saw that the pimp was in the room—and he was holding a twelve-inch butcher knife.

The man smiled, but it wasn't friendly. "Now," he said, "you're gonna die!"

Before I could react, he thrust the knife hard at my chest. I winced and felt a hot surge through my body. I looked down and saw the knife blade plunged completely inside me, the handle stopped against my chest. The blade had missed my heart by a quarter inch.

The woman screamed and kept screaming.

The pimp yanked out the knife and thrust it at me again. The blow was aimed at my head, but I jerked back. This time the blade entered my neck and came out the other side. It severed my jugular vein. Though I didn't know it at the time, when the jugular is completely cut, most people bleed out in less than four minutes.

Adrenaline shot through me. *I've got to fight my way out of here!*

As my attacker jerked the knife out a second time, I punched with my left hand, hitting him in the upper chest and throat. He started to fall. With my right arm, I instinctively hooked the man's leg and pulled. His head hit the floor with a loud thud.

I saw my chance. I leapt over his body, which blocked my way to the back door and freedom. But he wasn't finished with me yet. As I jumped, he stabbed a third time. This time the blade sliced into my liver.

I continued my forward motion until I reached the door. I turned the handle, but it didn't give. I'd locked it! I was running out of time. The pimp was getting up from the floor, and I was too panicked to unlock the door and remove the chain lock.

Knowing I didn't have a second to spare, my adrenaline pumping, I stepped back, lowered my shoulder, and rammed the door with all the strength I could find. It broke from its hinges and fell down flat.

Half running, half stumbling, I raced toward the Camaro, where a horrified Danny sat in the driver's seat. Danny later told me he'd heard the loud noise and banging sounds from inside the room and didn't know what to think or do. As he squinted, trying to see in the darkness, the door suddenly broke loose and there I stood, naked and covered in blood, the lone light swinging from the ceiling behind me. He said it looked like something from a horror movie.

> I made it to the car and stumbled against the hood, yelling, "Get out of here!"

I made it to the car and stumbled against the hood, yelling, "Get out of here!" I ran across the street and into a parking lot next to a deserted theater, where I wrapped my arms around a metal light pole. Slowly, my strength fading, I slid to the ground, smearing the light pole with blood.

I stared up at the stars, gasping for breath, choking on my own blood. My heart was pounding so hard it felt like it would bust out of my chest. I'd suffered three devastating wounds. Any one of them was enough to kill me, and I had no doubt I was dying. A friend had died from a single ice pick wound to the stomach. I couldn't imagine I'd survive this.

Of all the things a dying young man might think of in his final moments, a brief conversation with someone I barely knew is not what I would have expected. But as I clung to what was left of my life, one sentence from that conversation entered my mind, clearly and calmly. They were words I'd heard just two weeks before.

I'd been at home when there was a knock at the door, and I'd answered it. There stood a slim fellow in glasses, maybe seventeen years old.

"B-B-Bill," the visitor stammered, "everything you're looking for can be found in Jesus."

I stared at him without speaking. "I gotta go," he said nervously and ran away.

I hadn't known what to make of it. Only later did I learn that God had prompted this young man to come to my door and share his faith. He'd been in a church meeting when the speaker challenged the young people to witness to the most "lost" person they knew. Though he didn't know me well, this boy felt he had to talk to me. He wondered if anyone had ever told me about Jesus.

At the time, I just shook my head and tried to forget about it. But that boy messed me up. Have you ever had a song stuck in your head? That's what it was like for me. Every day, whenever it was quiet, his words kept replaying in my mind: "Everything you're looking for can be found in Jesus."

> **As I clung to the light pole and anticipated the end of my life, the words from that strange encounter came back to me again.**

As I clung to the light pole and anticipated the end of my life, the words from that strange encounter came back to me again.

I wasn't a churchgoing guy. I didn't read the Bible, and I'd never prayed in my life. But I decided it was now or never. "Jesus," I cried out as I choked on my own blood, "help me. Save me. Please forgive me of my sins. Help me, God. Please save me."

I heard Danny trying to start the Camaro. Tires squealed, and the roar of the engine grew louder until he skidded to a stop beside me. I somehow managed to get to the car and dived in the passenger seat. "Get me to a hospital!" I shouted.

Danny raced to the Columbus Medical Center, which fortunately for me was only half a block away. At the emergency room entrance, I used the last bit of adrenaline I had left to walk up to an orderly who'd stepped outside for a cigarette break. He had his back turned and didn't see me coming. I wrapped my arms around him and choked out, "I need some help, buddy."

The orderly grabbed me, ran inside, threw me onto a gurney, and rushed me inside the emergency room, leaving behind a trail of blood. Three doctors immediately came in. One was Philip Brewer, a renowned cardiothoracic vascular surgeon who happened to have stayed past the end of his shift that day. Another was Larry Brightwell, a trauma specialist who'd served in the Army Medical Corps in Vietnam. The third was Robert Lightenor, an emergency room physician.

One of the doctors examined my throat. "Get the district attorney up here," he said. "This boy's been stabbed to death. His jugular vein's completely cut. He's not dead yet, but he will be before the DA gets here."

I was still conscious and heard everything he'd said. I knew my time was almost up.

Doug Pullen, assistant district attorney, happened to be riding for the first time with a police officer that night. He showed up minutes later. He said it was easy to find the right room; he just followed the trail of blood. "It looked," he said later, "like someone had taken a bucket of red paint and poured it down the hallway." After being told I was about to die, Pullen asked me a few questions about what happened.

A doctor soon interrupted. "I have to start surgery now." Then the anesthesia kicked in, and I was out.

Second Life

I regained consciousness eleven hours later. I didn't have the strength to move, but I could turn my head enough to take in my surroundings. I was in a hospital bed hooked up to all kinds of machines. Through the open door, I could see policemen standing in the hallway outside my room and nurses walking by. Then memories from the night before came flooding back. It hadn't been a dream—I was supposed to be dead! But this didn't look like heaven or hell. It was the hospital. Somehow, I was alive. As I replayed the events that had led me here, I remembered. *You prayed and asked God to come into your life and save you.*

> **I regained consciousness eleven hours later.**

It was the only possible explanation for the fact that I was still alive. I was deeply humbled. I felt I didn't deserve to be alive. I also felt that I was too sinful and unworthy to have any favor or mercy from God. I always thought he loved only the good people. I prayed again: "God, thank you for what you did. Thank you for helping me. But you don't know what you got last night. You got somebody you can't use or do anything with. If you don't ever want to have anything to do with me or hear from me again, I understand. I won't bother you anymore."

The strangest feeling came over me in that moment. I felt both a peace in my heart and a sense of God's loving amusement, almost as if he were chuckling at my naivete.

Then, to my surprise, I sensed a response to my prayer.

Bill, just do what I tell you to do from now on. Let me do the rest.

It was a turning point, the beginning of my second life.

A few days into my recovery, I suddenly had the most intense hunger for the Bible. I wasn't even a reader of regular books, but once I found a Gideon Bible in the hospital nightstand, it was like the greatest gift I'd ever received. In another sign of God's surprising interest in me, a nurse who noticed my craving for the Bible asked me what I was reading one day.

"Spasms," I said.

"Spasms?" she asked.

We eventually figured out that what I thought was *spasms* was actually the book of Psalms. When it came to spiritual matters, I was totally clueless.

Over the next few days, she started to come in thirty minutes early for her shift so she could spend time reading and explaining the Bible to me. When she got to the story about Jesus walking on water, I protested.

"Hold on," I said. "What do you mean, he walked on water? Nobody walks on water."

"He saved you, didn't He?" she said.

I decided she had a point. "Read on."

The more I learned about the Bible, the hungrier I was to learn more about God. It was the most amazing thing. The doctors were amazed too—not so much at my spiritual transformation, but because I was still breathing. The night of the attack, a doctor told the assistant district attorney, Doug Pullen, that I wouldn't make it until morning. In the morning, doctors said I was still alive, but it was unlikely I would survive. The next morning, Pullen was told that I might live, but if I did, I would have no mental capacity. I'd been without oxygen for too long.

Instead, though I'd lost eight pints of blood and required over one hundred stitches, I made a complete recovery. I am one of a handful of people in the world who have survived a severed jugular vein.

Six months after I was stabbed, the pimp was arrested, charged with aggravated assault, and sentenced to ten years in prison. His plan, forced on his wife, had been to lure an unsuspecting teen to the house. While in the car with Danny, he'd said he was going to take a walk to have a cigarette. Instead, he moved quickly to the front of the house, grabbed a butcher knife as he passed through the kitchen, and waited for the signal from his wife. When the light went out, he slipped into the room through the unlocked door, intending to kill me and steal my money. But the would-be murderers didn't count on my left hook, much less my deathbed prayer and miraculous recovery.

"The only reason I can give you for Bill Purvis being alive right now is that God had a purpose for him," Doug Pullen later said in an interview recorded for our church. "He wanted him to fulfill that purpose. Even the doctors will tell you that this is one they can chalk up to God, not to anything they did."

You Don't Have to Wait

> **"The only reason I can give you for Bill Purvis being alive right now is that God had a purpose for him."**

I should have died that night in Columbus, but God healed me— physically and spiritually—and gave me another chance. Everything I have and cherish today—my wife, my children and grandchildren, my friends, my church, my home—is the result of what God did for me beginning that night. The only explanation for my continued existence is that God spared my life so he could show me his amazing grace. There is a beautiful passage from the Psalms that captures my story and always reminds me of that miracle when I read it:

> He brought me up out of the pit of destruction, out of the miry clay,
> And he set my feet upon a rock making my footsteps firm.
> He put a new song in my mouth, a song of praise to our God;
> Many will see and fear
> And will trust in the Lord. (Psalm 40:2–3)

It took a violent attack and a miraculous recovery for me to realize that God holds my destiny in his hands. But you don't have to be like me. You don't have to wait until you're staring death in the face to discover the path to your purpose.

God loves you, and he really does have a unique and amazing plan for you too. If you're willing to join me on this adventure, I want to help you break through the obstacles you face—outside of you and within you—to uncover the destiny God imagined for you before you were born. I can't tell you what your purpose is, but I can promise you that it's far more exciting and fulfilling than anything you've experienced in life so far.

Let's continue the journey together.

STORY 45

Lu Ann Topovski

YEARS AGO, I was invited to a church which often had speakers come in from all over the country. There was a prophet from California coming to this church, and I didn't know if I wanted to go because I had experienced some people taking the gifts of the spirit out of context. I am very protective when it comes to the Lord and the gifts of the Spirit, as they are sacred to me. I've never liked it when believers were led astray by people trying to produce the gifts. They can't. The move of the Spirit is powerful when we have a relationship with God. So in the spirit of openness, I went to the meeting. When I heard the message and saw many people healed and prophesied over, I knew the prophet was for real. I also knew I wanted to go back the next night.

After the service, I was able to shake hands with the prophet before leaving the church. I told him I was going to do my best to come back the next night but needed to find a babysitter. I told him if I came back the next day, "I wanted a word from the Lord." He smiled and said, "I'll be listening." As fate would have it, I found a babysitter, and I returned the next night.

At the beginning of the service, the prophet asked if he could borrow someone's sunglasses. Everyone was scrambling for their sunglasses. I offered him my prescription sunglasses, and he said, "These will do." Then he walked to the front of the church, looked over at his keyboardist and said, "Didn't I tell you that whoever's sunglasses I use tonight, they would receive a word from the Lord?"

> "I wanted a word from the Lord."

His keyboardist said, "Yes, you did say that."

The prophet looked at me and said to me, "Aren't you the person who said to me last night that you needed to find a babysitter in order to come tonight? And if you came, you wanted a word from the Lord?"

With a smile, I said, "Yes."

Considering there were hundreds of people the night before and another packed house that night, I was happy he remembered me. In my spirit, I knew it was God who remembered me and my prayer request. Midway through the service, he started calling people up to the front and started to prophesy and/or pray over them. It was amazing and powerful. He then called me up front. I was nervous. I walked on stage, and he put his hand on my head and said, "The Lord says, 'You will see as you have never seen before. For tonight I have anointed you and called you to be a prophetess of the Lord.'" I don't remember what else was said, but I remember someone catching me as I fell backward. I eventually got up and went back to my seat.

That same night, the prophet was asking if anyone knew a Peggy Ann? He said, "First name Peggy, middle name Ann." No one answered. He said, "She has a granddaughter in the hospital, and they don't know if she will live or die." I knew my aunt Peg had a granddaughter in the hospital who was very sick. My mom had called me the day before and asked me to pray for her. She said it didn't look good, and they didn't know if she would live or die. As I was thinking of this, the prophet said it again. "Does anyone know a Peggy? Or Peggy Ann? I'm hearing the Lord say, 'First name Peggy, middle name Ann.'"

Still in a daze from what just happened to me, I said, "I have an aunt Peg, sometimes they call her Peggy. I don't know her middle name, but my middle name is Ann. She has a granddaughter in the hospital who is very sick. They don't know what is going to happen to her."

He said, "That's it! The Lord says, she will live and not die!"

I called my mom and Aunt Peg the next day. I told them what happened and what was said. I told Aunt Peg that I would continue to pray for her and her granddaughter. That was over twenty years ago. Her granddaughter is alive and well today.

Ever since I was a little girl, I prayed for God to heal my eyes. I had astigmatism and always wanted to wake up and see perfectly. After the prophetic word I received, I wondered if that was meant by the words, "You will see as you have never seen before." I wondered if I was going to receive a miracle and literally be able to see physically with my eyes.

> "You will see as you have never seen before."

But that wasn't it. I began to have visions. I began to have vivid dreams. I was speaking in tongues more. I was interpreting more. I felt the discernment of the Holy Spirit. It was powerful. I also felt the enemy trying to attack me and my family members.

I became part of an ecumenical women's church group called the End Times Handmaidens. These women were from every denominational church in the Akron area. It was refreshing to have Methodists, Assemblies of God, Church of Christ, Baptists, Catholics, Pentecostals, Brethren, and nondenominations in one room with one accord. We all spoke in tongues, prophesied, and did spiritual warfare for each other, the city, the state, the nation, Jerusalem, and the world. It was one of the most exciting times in my life because we felt the movement and presence of the Holy Spirit every time we met.

During this time, I saw some amazing miracles. One of the first miracles was my sister, Michelle. I call her Mick. She was in an accident, going about thirty-five miles an hour when someone hit her and completely demolished her car. There was no way she should have survived this accident, as her car was smashed and the metal was compacted into a little ball. The fire department and ambulance had to use the Jaws of Life to break her out of her car. They Life-Flighted her to Cleveland Metro Hospital.

I remember praying for her life to be spared and for her body to be healed. She was in the best place. We had a bit of a falling out just prior to her accident, but I remember visiting her in the hospital and praying for her restoration. She made it through all surgeries and is physically OK today, even though she has a few metal pieces in her leg. That was over twenty years ago. What was miraculous is she had no ill feelings about the people who hit her

> **What was miraculous is she had no ill feelings about the people who hit her car.**

car. She knew in her spirit that everything was going to be OK. And she was right.

Shortly after this I began singing with our praise and worship band. I love to sing and enjoyed being a part of the band. However, after a few months, God said, "I didn't call you to sing, I called you to preach." Although I was devastated, I was obedient to his word to me. I began leading Bible studies, which turned into sermons. I felt like I was in heaven. The anointing was strong, and I loved researching the Bible. I became so close to God and my discernment became stronger. I remember laying hands on various people and praying for them. They would get healed, and I would give the glory to God.

Another miracle was when a friend of mine from Texas came to visit. We met while attending College in Columbus. She moved to Texas and I moved to the Akron area, but we always kept in touch. We talked often on the phone and she had recently been diagnosed with MS. She asked the elders of her church to pray James 5:13–15 BSB, which says, "Is any one of you suffering? He should pray. Is anyone cheerful? He should sing praises. Is anyone of you sick? He should call the elders of the church to pray over him and anoint him with oil in the name of the Lord. And the prayer offered in faith will restore the one who is sick. The Lord will raise him up. If he has sinned, he will be forgiven."

Then she called me and told me she wanted to come to Ohio and have me lay hands on her to receive the baptism of the Holy Spirit. She came and we prayed. I anointed her head with oil and prayed over her to receive the gift of speaking in tongues. She began to speak in tongues. We also commanded and prayed for the MS to leave her body.

In fact, all the elders at my church prayed for her complete healing from MS. I spoke in tongues and interpreted. She went back to Texas and the MS symptoms went away. She felt like God was telling her, "Forty." She knew it meant something but didn't know what exactly. Even after she had been prayed for by her church and mine and her symptoms started diminishing, her doctor still would not un-diagnose her—for three years. Eventually, she was undiagnosed of MS.

While she was attending her church in Texas one day, God said, "Lea." She thought it was her husband, and she turned to him and said, "What?" Mike (her husband) said he didn't say anything. This happened two more times. The third time she heard, "Lea." She said, "What is it, Lord?" He told her that he was the one who healed her of the MS. He said for her to look at the date. It was forty months to the day in which she was diagnosed with MS.

My friend Lea is the first person in the world who has been undiagnosed from MS. There have been others undiagnosed since, but their remission has been with the help of medicine or other modalities. That was almost twenty years ago.

About a year later, I entered a graduate program at Ashland Theological Seminary. It was right around this time when my brother George was mowing a steep hill. The lawnmower turned over onto him as he was mowing. They took him to the emergency room and during the MRIs, CT scans, x-rays, and blood work, they discovered five cancerous tumors in his brain. The doctors only gave him a few weeks to live, and he opted to have a risky surgery. I decided that I would pray for him while I mowed the lawn. It took me an hour and half to mow our lawn, and I decided to speak in tongues for my brother during his surgery. I also prayed in English for God to heal my brother and dissolve the tumors.

After mowing the lawn, I called my mom to see how George was doing. My mom said that once the doctor got into George's brain, instead of there being cancerous tumors, they were cysts. The doctor said he had never seen anything like this before. He sent George home nine days after the surgery, but then he was back the very next day. This is when he died and went to heaven then came back to share what God showed him. (You can read the rest of George's amazing events in story 23.)

While attending Ashland Seminary, I had the pleasure of being among believers from over fifty different Christian denominations. This excited me so much because I felt like I was home with my spiritual family. We did not all agree in certain areas of theology but if there was a dispute, we would discuss it in the classroom. We would often take the discussion back to the original context or language of Hebrew or Greek to get clarity. We had discussions about gifts of the spirit, husbands and wives, women in ministry, men being the head of the household, water baptism, Holy Spirit baptism, and so much more. This was heaven to me because there was clarity in how some man-made traditions and religions skewed what was originally taught in the scriptures.

> **I believed that what I was learning in seminary should be taught at every pulpit.**

I believed that what I was learning in seminary should be taught at every pulpit. My classmates had the opportunity to share what they learned, and many of them did. However, some had other rules and regulations they needed to follow.

Many religions have certain protocols and religious belief systems pastors need to agree to in order to pastor in that denomination. When we believe the rules of the religion we want to serve in ministry, that is fantastic. We feel an alignment. We are being obedient in the move of the Holy Spirit in our lives. Other times, we might not agree 100 percent, but out of convenience or not wanting to push back, we compromise. This is when our integrity is called into play, and we unfortunately give in to man-made religious rules. It's unfortunate, but it happens.

Not that traditions or religions intentionally do this, but in Christian history, we learned that, over time, scripture was watered down to format into religions. Due to certain desires of wanting control of the people, the pulpit ministry was watered down or skewed to fit the religion. Many things have changed from the dark ages, and as far as I know, no one is paying for their loved ones to go to heaven these days. However, it did happen.

Those of us who attended ATS knew we had an opportunity to change things in our churches to the original intent in several controversial issues. It takes courage, faith, and desire to be obedient to the Holy Spirit to make this call. This is freedom in the Spirit, not bondage to a religion. This is not always easy to do because some people fear for not being able to provide for themselves or their family. What we must remember is that fear is not only a liar, it is a spirit. "For God has not given us the spirit of fear, but of power and of love and of a sound mind," 2 Timothy 1:7 NIV.

If anyone is feeling fear, we have the spiritual authority and right to bind it, tell it to go to hell and ask God for clarity, and power, over our situation. Those who are strong in their faith do this all the time, and everyone else can do it as well. Those who truly love our Lord Jesus and have a relationship with him, know this is true and it works. We overcome our spiritual enemy with the blood of the Lamb (Jesus Christ) and the words we speak (Proverbs 18:21 and Revelation 12:11). The ones with this faith and courage are the ones who speak up, even when it isn't popular.

I'm very careful when I bring this up because, like David in the Bible, before he was king, he would not harm or hurt God's anointed. At a certain time, King Saul was pursuing David in order to kill him. Saul was anointed as the first king of Israel, and David knew this. He was not going to go against God or who he anointed, even while Saul chased him throughout the country. He had an opportunity to kill Saul while he was in a cave but chose not to do so. Instead, he cut a piece of Saul's garment to show he could have killed him but chose not to harm him.

First Samuel 24:6 NIV says, "The LORD forbid that I should do this thing to my lord, the LORD's anointed, to put out my hand against him, seeing he is the LORD's anointed."

It is this scripture that I try to remember when given the opportunity to harm or hurt God's anointed with words or otherwise. I know who they are, and even when they have tried on numerous occasions to hurt, crush, or kill me, I do my best not to harm God's anointed. Is it easy? Not always. But this is where my integrity is developed and strengthened. Do I make mistakes? Yes, I do. Sometimes doozies. But I know my God will never leave me nor forsake me. When I acknowledge what I have done wrong, I am forgiven and move on from there. That's the best I can do. That's the best any of us can do—stay true to who he has called us to be and stay true to each assignment he places before us. With the help and strength of God, that is what I intend to do. This strengthens my personal relationship with him.

It is not our place to harm people; however, it is our responsibility to love them and speak the truth even if we are the only one with the insight or knowledge. When we are true to ourselves and do what we know is right and what the Lord is telling us to do then we are not only being obedient, we are being who God created us to be. This journey of obedience is often an adventure, but we receive blessings and often a great reward. This is walking in the kingdom of God. When we, "seek first the kingdom of God and his righteousness, all these things are added to you [us]" (Matthew 6:33 NIV, emphasis mine).

> **It is not our place to harm people; however, it is our responsibility to love them and speak the truth even if we are the only one with the insight or knowledge.**

Matthew 28:18 NLT:

"I have been given complete authority in heaven and on earth. Therefore, go and make disciples of all the nations, baptizing them in the name of the Father and the Son and the Holy Spirit. Teach these new disciples to obey all the commands I have given to you. And be sure of this: I am with you always, even to the end of the age."

Writing Your Story...

Everyone has a story. We would like to invite you, our reader, to take the time to write your story on the following blank pages. If you would like to share your story with us, please submit it to our website or email to : <u>Luanntopovski@outlook.com</u>. Please write, "My Story" in the subject line. Who knows, maybe your story will be selected to be in our next book.

Write on...